The Reproductive Unconscious in Medieval and Early Modern England

Medieval History and Culture
Volume 13

STUDIES IN
MEDIEVAL HISTORY AND CULTURE

edited by
Francis G. Gentry
Professor of German
Pennsylvania State University

A ROUTLEDGE SERIES

OTHER BOOKS IN THIS SERIES

1. "AND THEN THE END WILL COME"
Early Latin Christian Interpretations of the Opening of the Seven Seals
Douglas W. Lumsden

2. TOPOGRAPHIES OF GENDER IN MIDDLE HIGH GERMAN ARTHURIAN ROMANCE
Alexandra Sterling-Hellenbrand

3. CHRISTIAN, SARACEN AND GENRE IN MEDIEVAL FRENCH LITERATURE
Imagination and Cultural Interaction in the French Middle Ages
Lynn Tarte Ramey

4. WORD OUTWARD
Medieval Perspectives on the Entry into Language
Corey Marvin

5. JUSTICE & THE SOCIAL CONTEXT OF EARLY MIDDLE HIGH GERMAN LITERATURE
Robert G. Sullivan

6. MARRIAGE FICTIONS IN OLD FRENCH SECULAR NARRATIVES, 1170–1250
A Critical Re-evaluation of the Courtly Love Debates
Keith Nickolaus

7. WHERE TROUBADOURS WERE BISHOPS
The Occitania of Folc of Marseille (c. 1150–1231)
Nichole M. Schulman

8. JOHN CASSIAN AND THE READING OF EGYPTIAN MONASTIC CULTURE
Steven D. Driver

9. CHOOSING NOT TO MARRY
Women and Autonomy in the Katherine Group
Julie Hassel

10. FEMININE FIGURAE
Representations of Gender in Religious Texts by Medieval German Women Writers
Rebecca L.R. Garber

11. BODIES OF PAIN
Suffering in the Works of Hartmann von Aue
Scott E. Pincikowski

12. THE LITERAL SENSE AND THE GOSPEL OF JOHN IN LATE MEDIEVAL COMMENTARY AND LITERATURE
Mark Hazard

THE REPRODUCTIVE UNCONSCIOUS IN MEDIEVAL AND EARLY MODERN ENGLAND

Jennifer Wynne Hellwarth

LONDON AND NEW YORK

First published 2002 by
Routledge

2 Park Square, Milton Park, Abingdon, Oxon OX14 4RN
711 Third Avenue, New York, NY 10017, USA

Routledge is an imprint of the Taylor & Francis Group, an informa business

First issued in paperback 2016

Copyright © 2002 Taylor & Francis.

All rights reserved. No part of this book may be reprinted or reproduced or utilised in any form or by any electronic, mechanical, or other means, now known or hereafter invented, including photocopying and recording, or in any information storage or retrieval system, without permission in writing from the publishers.

Notice:
Product or corporate names may be trademarks or registered trademarks, and are used only for identification and explanation without intent to infringe.

Library of Congress Cataloging-in-Publication Data

Hellwarth, Jennifer Wynne, 1961–
  The reproductive unconscious in medieval and early modern England / by Jennifer Wynne Hellwarth.
    p. cm. — (Studies in medieval history and culture ; v. 13)
  Includes bibliographical references (p.) and index.
  1. English literature—Middle English, 1100–1500—History and criticism. 2. Childbirth in literature. 3. English literature—Early modern, 1500–1700—History and criticism. 4. Literature and medicine—England—History. 5. Women and literature—England—History. 6. Human reproduction in literature. 7. Subconsciousness in literature. 8. Virginity in literature. 9. Sex role in literature. I. Title. II. Series.
  PR275.C48 H45 2002
  820.9´354—dc21
                                                           2002004327

ISBN 13: 978-0-415-94152-5 (hbk)
ISBN 13: 978-1-138-98518-6 (pbk)

Series Editor Foreword

Far from providing just a musty whiff of yesteryear, research in Medieval Studies enters the new century as fresh and vigorous as never before. Scholars representing all disciplines and generations are consistently producing works of research of the highest caliber, utilizing new approaches and methodologies. Volumes in the Medieval History and Culture series will include studies on individual works and authors of Latin and vernacular literatures, historical personalities and events, theological and philosophical issues, and new critical approaches to medieval literature and culture.

Momentous changes have occurred in Medieval Studies in the past thirty years in teaching as well as in scholarship. Thus the goal of the Medieval History and Culture series is to enhance research in the field by providing an outlet for monographs by scholars in the early stages of their careers on all topics related to the broad scope of Medieval Studies, while at the same time pointing to and highlighting new directions that will shape and define scholarly discourse in the future.

Francis G. Gentry

Contents

Preface	xi
Introduction: Literacy, Ritual, and the Reproductive Unconscious	xv
1. "I wyl wright of women prevy sekenesse": Female Textual and Birth Communities and the History of Women's Medical Texts	1
2. Theologized Maternity in Julian of Norwich's *Book of Showings*	25
3. A Very Maternal Mysticism: Images of Childbirth and Its Rituals in *The Book of Margery Kempe*	43
4. "with grievous groanes & deepe sighes": Female Textual and Birth Communities in *The Monument of Matrones*	61
Notes	89
Select Bibliography	111
Index	123

Preface

The project of trying to unravel the matrix of female literacy, childbirth, and devotional practices necessarily requires an interdisciplinary approach, one that draws on medical, social, and literary history. As a scholar of literature I recognize the considerable challenges of the task I have sought to undertake in drawing on these disparate fields. Therefore, I have relied on documentary work done by medical and social historians, as well as literary historians and critics, in constructing interpretive paradigms. I use these paradigms to examine more "literary" devotional texts, such as Julian of Norwich's *Book of Showings*, Margery Kempe's *The Book of Margery Kempe*, and Thomas Bentley's *Monument of Matrones*, in relation to more "medical" texts, such as *Trotula* and Thomas Raynald's *Byrth of Mankynde*. Through this process, I seek to show the dynamics of the negotiation of women's voices around the idea of female reproductive body as it is mediated and imagined through these female literacy, devotional texts, and medical practices. At times the works I take up offer images of female textual communities and an authoritative social "voice"; sometimes the voice seeks to participate in or enable the community; sometimes it seeks to infiltrate and disrupt it. While we cannot know whether the descriptions and imaginations of these female textual communities are representative of those who actually acquired and used these texts, they do infer a potential and desired, if not true, readership. Thus, these texts give us a sense of a female literacy that is both secret, yet culturally valuable.

In preparing this manuscript for publication I hope to participate in the ongoing discussion of what is a project of a growing number of literary scholars including Margaret Ferguson, Frances Dolan, and Eve Sanders, who study literacy using gender as a category of examination.[1] By adding gender to the mix, these scholars challenge the more traditional definitions of literacy such as those established by David Cressy's influential *Literacy and the Social Order*.[2] They have sought instead to define literacies by exploring the multiple ways in which the "products of a culture can be acquired and transmitted."[3] Recent contributions emerging after I finished this manuscript include critical work about gender and literacy and women's medical history. I should also mention Ferguson's *Dido's Daughters: Literacy, Gender, and Empire in Early Modern France and England*, and Gail McMurray Gibson's article "Scene and Obscene: Seeing and Performing Late Medieval Childbirth," both of which engage in the kinds of literary and historical analysis to which I aspire.[4] Another recent significant contribution to the field of women's medical history is Monica Green's edition and translation of the *Trotula*. Her text establishes for the first time a "standardized ensemble" out of the multiple *Trotula* manuscripts that circulated throughout Europe from the late twelfth through the fifteenth centuries. She has also contributed multiple critical works on gender and medical literacy.[5] By imagining less traditional forms of female literacy, these scholars have allowed for the possibility of interrogating the cultural currency these broader forms of literacy carried.[6] I hope that my more modest work, which examines cultural constructions as well as practices of medieval and early modern female devotional, childbirth, and literacy communities, will offer us opportunities to continue redefining what it meant to be literate and female.

As with most projects, this book could not have been completed without the diligent and constant support provided by family, friends, and colleagues. Many thanks belong to Margaret W. Ferguson, who continues to encourage and inspire me to "grab the tiger by the tail," and whose class on "Renaissance Women of Letters" forever changed the way I thought about literature. I also owe much to L. O. Aranye Frandenburg's brilliant and penetrating questions and insights, and to Michael O'Connell, who energetically and generously gave his attention to the project. To my dear friends and colleagues Roze Hentschell, Kate Koppelman, and Kathy Lavezzo I owe a debt of gratitude for their tireless support, and for religiously and compassionately reading drafts, and without whom this book could have not been written. I also owe untold thanks to Carol Braun Pasternack. As an advisor, she devoted hours of her time and intellectual energy during countless conversations; she labored over draft after draft with a sharp eye for detail, offering extraordinary insights along with encouraging words. As a friend, she believed in me even when I didn't believe in myself, and she continues to inspire me with her inimitable calm and infectious humor.

Many thanks go to E. Cook, Anne Deane, Tracy Kirst, Gary Monheit, Yuka Persico, Amy Rabbino, Judith Rose, Michelle Shapiro, and Spencer Weiner for providing my family with loving attention and diversions over the years. I also wish to thank my father, Steven Dorfman, for all his good advice (even the advice I didn't take), and for always believing in me no matter what. He, Beverley Dorfman, Abby Hellwarth, Robert Hellwarth and Theresia de Vroom provided gracious guidance and ever-generous understanding and support. My two children, Sutter and Camryn Hellwarth, helped me keep things in perspective and brought me great joy and love every day. Finally, to my husband, Ben Hellwarth, I owe my deepest gratitude and admiration for tolerating the at times intolerable, for relentlessly and lovingly supporting my every endeavor, and for being an extraordinary writer, reader, father, and partner in all things.

Introduction
Literacy, Ritual, and the Reproductive Unconscious

IN SEARCH OF . . . THE REPRODUCTIVE UNCONSCIOUS

While many scholars have considered the complexities of sex and sexuality in literary texts, childbirth is a central experience that has been overlooked in literary scholarship.[1] Feminist critics have long concerned themselves with the representation of the sexing and the sexualization of the female body. They have been interested in the ways in which women have been constructed as sexual objects and have been gendered "female." In particular, medieval and early modern feminist scholars such as Sarah Beckwith, Carolyn Bynum, Carolyn Dinshaw, Karma Lochrie, Margaret Ferguson, Patricia Parker and Constance Jordan, to name a few, have been interrogating the scene where the "voice" of the woman seems to begin to be heard.[2] There has been particular interest in female affective religious piety in the thirteenth through fifteenth centuries, as well as in the burgeoning number of texts by women in the late-sixteenth and early-seventeenth centuries. While there has been considerable scholarship recently on the construction and performative nature of gender and sexuality, and while some attention has been given to the construction of sexuality in relationship to medieval and early modern medical notions of women, as of this writing, no extensive study has examined medieval and early modern notions of reproduction and childbirth.[3] This is in part because the rituals and practices of medieval and early modern childbirth are difficult to track due to the lack of traditional documentary evidence. Therefore, even though interrelated to sexuality and gender, reproduction and childbirth have been subsumed under these topics, or even ignored altogether.

Drawing together social and medical history and literary studies, this book examines social practices and metaphorical representations of childbirth in late medieval and early modern obstetrical and gynecological treatises, and in devotional texts written either by or for women. I show how medieval and early modern men and women had to negotiate a conflict between the ideological and material need of the culture for them to procreate, and the ideological injunction that they remain virginal and nonprocreative. This conflict was negotiated on a social level through instructional manuals, midwives, and gossips; obstetrical and gynecological manuals in particular directly addressed reproductive practices. However, in literary representations, parturition was repressed or distorted. Medieval and early modern men's and women's experiences and apprehensions of childbirth, and their difficulty expressing the experience, were in part a result of the conflicting discourses of virginity and procreation and the inherent physical dangers of childbirth. These repressions and distortions have led me to theorize the existence of a "reproductive unconscious." Although not Marxist in its theoretical underpinnings, my work in this book draws upon Frederic Jameson's notion of the "political unconscious" as a basis for the reproductive unconscious. In his chapter "On Interpretation: Literature as a Socially Symbolic Act," Jameson argues that texts mirror diachronic social struggles (particularly class struggles). The culture then "resolves" these conflicts through literary discourses.[4] I argue, then, the existence of a reproductive unconscious in the culture, which emerges in particularly arresting ways in the devotional texts that sought to teach virginity and prescribe enclosure. These texts mirror and seek to "resolve" conflicts around the work of the potentially procreative body. While devotional texts in the middle ages used images of childbirth metaphorically to describe spiritual states, early modern texts inverted this relationship, using sacred images to allay the fears of women in labor. In addition, my study of the articulation of maternity and birth rituals shows a complicated, overlapping relationship between female birth, devotional, and textual communities, and suggests that the transmission of knowledge among women in medieval and early modern England was more intricate than we have envisioned it previously. In its movement from medieval to early modern texts, the book's documentation of historical changes and continuities seeks in part to repudiate conventional paradigms of periodization, and, in its thematics, brings women's creativity into the center of cultural inquiry.

THE CHAPTERS

Chapter One begins with a brief description of late medieval and early modern, male-formulated medical notions of women as a background for understanding obstetrical and gynecological texts generated from female experience. In it, I contextualize the production and implied audiences for the medieval "Sekenesse of Wymmen," the Middle English version of the female-authored *Trotula*, and the two early modern obstetrical manuals, Eucharius Rösslin's *The Rose Garden for Pregnant Women and Midwives* and Thomas Raynald's translation of *De partu hominis*, *The Byrth of Mankynde*. These texts express the physiologic notions of reproduction and the handling of childbirth. These manuals also suggest the existence

Introduction *xvii*

and role of female textual communities in childbirth, and, in the case of the early modern texts, show ways in which men sought to manage childbirth themselves. Finally, I turn to birth rituals as implied in these and other texts.

Chapter Two shifts focus from the social management of childbirth to the social management of virgins and the more "literary" negotiations and representations of childbirth found in devotional texts. I first look at two male-authored medieval instructional manuals intended for women, *Hali Meidenhad*, which argues strongly for female virginity by invoking, among other things, the horrors of childbirth, and *Ancrene Wisse*, which guides women in the everyday practice of an anchorite. These texts help to explain the terms of the conflict between discourses of virginity and maternity in Julian of Norwich's *Book of Showings*. Julian uses images of God and Christ as maternal figures to represent God's loving yet instructive relationship to mankind. I read these images as an expression of the reproductive unconscious in which Julian, through repeatedly describing God and Christ as "our only mother," seeks to resolve the conflicting ideologies of virginity and maternity through masculinizing them.

Chapter Three turns from the revelations of the enclosed Julian of Norwich to the "boisterous" spiritual expression of Margery in *The Book of Margery Kempe*. This chapter looks at how the *Book* negotiates the conflict between the female procreative body and the ideal virginal body through representations of Margery's spiritual practices. For example, I argue that while the text avoids discussion of Margery's own fourteen children, it enacts births and mothering in her visions of the Virgin Mary, St. Anne, and Elizabeth. I also argue that the friction between Margery's female voice and her male scribes generates the text's discontinuities and discomfort with female birth and textual communities. Finally, Chapter Four examines a text that few scholars have addressed, the late sixteenth-century *The Monument of Matrones*. Compiled and edited by Thomas Bentley, *Monument* presents devotional texts, prayers, and meditations by women. As in Kempe's book, certain sections point towards a discordance between the male editor and the female communities constructed through the contained prayers and meditations. But in contrast to its medieval counterparts, this text brings the women's own acts of childbirth directly into devotions and thereby both privileges childbirth as sacred to God and attempts to relocate these acts within a sacred structure that is also masculine.

"THE VOICES OF BOOKS"

In this introductory chapter, I propose the importance of three different kinds of female communities centered on the dissemination of knowledge: textual, devotional, and birth communities. Using current scholarship on orality, textual communities, and female literacy, I argue that these communities overlap and inform each other in their production and dissemination of knowledge. The subject of women authors and women's literacy in medieval and early modern England is a tricky matter to navigate. Although evidence is perhaps more ample than is commonly acknowledged, there is currently a limited set of sources and evidence of female authors, book owners, and women's literacy to be found within a limited range of evidence of medieval and early modern literacy in general.[5] While there is a very general consensus among scholars that, to some degree, the higher the class and the more urbane, the more likely a woman (or man, for that matter) was to be literate, the only sure thing is the all around uncertainty about the specific level of literacy among women across classes and geographical locations. Nonetheless, it is necessary to keep searching for clues to levels of literacy, and to try to pose questions and propose theories regarding the various definitions of literacy and textual communities, and specifically any distinctive forms of women's literacy, literature, and women's textual communities that might have been instrumental in cultural shifts such as the Reformation.

What I also seek to do in this chapter is to establish a model of a female "textual community," which I use as a paradigm for understanding the kinds of female birth communities that are implicated by the obstetrical and gynecological manuals taken up in the first chapter. I suggest some of the kinds of literacy practices women might have engaged in, as well as the kinds of texts women might have owned or had access to, to help to establish this model. To begin, I take the basic notion of a textual community from Brian Stock, who argues that "what was essential to a textual community was not a written version of a text, although that was sometimes present, but an individual, who, having mastered it, then utilized it for reforming a group's thought and action."[6] I modify Stocks's notion of textual community, which does not take into account gender, to be particular to women's textual practices in the medieval and early modern periods. This female textual community existed in relationship to female devotional communities and female birth communities.

Many critics have argued and agreed that defining the term "literacy" in medieval and early modern England is not a simple task; it defies the more modern (and relatively uncomplicated) definition of having the ability to read and write. In medieval terminology, a *litteratus* was someone learned in Latin, and an *illitteratus* was someone who was not learned in Latin. Eventually, *litteratus* and *illitteratus* came to be associated with the clergy and laity respectively.[7] But these terms were not used for describing literacy in the vernacular, or the various categories and levels of competence in both reading and writing, either in Latin or in the vernacular. It is therefore important to keep in mind, especially in terms of women who had reading and/or writing skills, the idea of "literacies" rather than literacy. That is to say, there are (and were) multiple ways in which the "products of a culture can be acquired and transmitted."[8] So, even though medieval and early

Introduction

modern women across the classes were often denied access to the education in reading and writing that their male counterparts had, there is evidence that these women managed to find ways to learn how to read and gain access to texts—particularly devotional texts. Additionally, fewer people learned to write than learned to read because it was more complicated to learn to write than to read, and it is generally accepted that if one didn't learn to read and write when one was young, it was likely not to happen at all.[9] This was particularly true for women; writing required many more implements and was generally part of an organized education system of which women were not necessarily a part. Further, it was not desirable that women should be able to compose.

Some women did learn to read, and even more were actively involved in textual communities. Lollard communities illustrate the ways in which women could gain access to literacy and the potential to form female textual communities. John Wycliffe (1328–84) was pivotal to burgeoning vernacular literacy through his enabling of the production of an English Language Wycliffite Bible. Wycliffe's role in the translation of the Gospel into English from Latin allowed for greater and broader access to these texts—including access by women.[10] The relatively widespread use of Bibles in the vernacular by families across all classes (and particularly by the poor) suggests literacy levels were increasing in general among all classes by the late Middle Ages.[11] In addition, the reception and use of the English Bible and other devotional texts did not necessarily demand as a high level of literacy as we might imagine. As long as one had access to texts through those that could read, or those who could re-create a text orally (a text didn't have to be written to function within a "textual community"), one functioned as having a certain degree of literacy.[12] As Margaret Aston argues, while all Lollards "were neither readers nor textual learners, a significant number were."[13] Women were particularly important textual learners, for they were involved in and responsible for the education of their children and families, and so we may imagine it was not uncommon for groups of women to gather around a "text," with one or so "literate" women disseminating its contents. And, as the case of Lollard women suggests, reading and information could be acquired in a number of situations.

The means by which women educated their own daughters through communal instruction, and the role they played as patrons of devotional texts together suggest a model of female textual communities.[14] Many women desired access to texts and information, and therefore gathered together for the purpose of not only reading devotional works, but also for communicating with relatives and friends at a distance (in the from of writing and reading letters), and for reading histories and literature. While reading, writing, and book ownership for women in the twelfth and thirteenth centuries seems to have been largely limited to the "cultural elite"—nuns from wealthy convents and royal or noble women—the late-fourteenth through early-sixteenth centuries witnessed a "massive" increase and diversification in female book ownership, of which the readership and ownership of literate nuns is the best documented.[15] But lay women who were not noble, according to Anne Clark Bartlett and Susan Groag Bell, also began to own and circulate texts during this period, at least in part because they were largely responsible for their children's early education. Wives and mothers "assisted in the dissemination of vernacular translations across Europe" as part of educating their children (Bartlett, 9–10). These vernacular translations, like those used and owned by monastic nuns, were by and large devotional texts.[16] There is also evidence that literacy among women in the fourteenth and fifteenth centuries was higher than has often been thought. Take, for example, the case of women in the Lollard movement—several of whom were imprisoned for activities related to their literacy.[17]

Throughout the late Middle Ages and the early modern period, more and more women not only owned books, but many noblewomen became patrons as well. And, as Bell has also argued, women became patrons of translations and productions of texts that had a great influence on literary and cultural developments, particularly in terms of the Reformation. This influence was shaped by the kinds of translations and texts these women chose to patronize, and the people to whom these texts might have ultimately been bequeathed. Women patrons themselves could make up a textual community in which they supported and promoted women's literacy through their patronage and authorship of certain texts intended for use by women. Bell argues that medieval women, "because of their inferior status in medieval Christian thought and their exclusion from scholarship and clerical life, had an even greater need for the mental and spiritual nourishment offered by books than men did...and as mothers they were the primary teachers of the next generation and acquired books as teaching texts" (Bell, 150). This acquisition of texts, of course, increased dramatically with the advent of the printing press, and with the increase in the availability of affordable books. While in the thirteenth and fourteenth centuries women seemed to have owned mostly devotional and instructional texts, in the fifteenth and early-sixteenth centuries, women owned a greater variety of books, including devotional books, conduct books, instructional manuals, political texts, and a variety of books designed for entertainment.[18]

In addition to women generally owning a greater variety and number of books, there were several important women patrons and translators of significant texts during the sixteenth century, including Catherine Parr, Margaret Roper, and the Cooke sisters, to name a few.[19] These women, like many medieval women before them, owned books and had a special relationship to the development of cultural change in Reformation England through the books they patronized and owned. Catherine Parr, for example, was part of a group of women who helped to popularize "protestant humanism through patronage of devotional manuals and theological translations for the edification of a mixed audience of elite and ordinary readers," thus bringing the theological study together with worship for an often specifically female textual community.[20] Several male humanists also had an impact on women's literacy in England beginning in the second quarter of the sixteenth century. The treatises and instructional manuals proffered by Thomas More, Erasmus, and Juan Luis Vives seemed, at least, to give a new opening and call to lay and, in particular, female literacy. Even when the more conservative religious (such as Thomas More) argued that literacy was not valuable for the masses and that salvation in fact did not depend upon the acquisition of literacy, the humanist and Reformation movement was still to educate noble women. But this education was a limited one, and very specifically oriented towards restricting women's behavior, especially as it related to religion (proper devotion) and domestic roles (proper motherhood). Humanistic scholarship for women put an emphasis on reading; girls would likely learn religion and reading, but not necessarily writing-maybe twice as many could read as write (Houston, 135). In addition, those women who did write were more likely to translate texts, not compose them, and literacy for the sake of good maternal conduct was emphasized.

It was not only the humanists who engaged in the literacy debate. Lay and female literacy had its roots as a political and religious weapon among Wycliffe followers and Lollards. Later, Catholic and Protestant groups alike tried to "win" both men and women into their folds through their respective church's particular relationship to literacy and devotional methods. Protestants actively associated themselves with literacy, and literacy was an integral part of the Protestant experience. Part of the lure of Protestantism, for women in particular, was this advertisement that those who could read were better prepared for salvation. Further, Protestants claimed literacy was a tool which could be used against Catholics. But writing (and reading) could also be used profanely. Women were prime targets of suspicion for the profane use of literacy, and so while the Reformation movement encouraged greater literacy particularly among women, it also brought strict policies about what was appropriate reading and what was appropriate writing (if any at all) for women.

Further, one of the most notable changes in devotion that came out of the Reformation movement was the dissolution of the monasteries, which had been used as sanctuaries for unmarried or religious women and men, and the waning of the Cult of the Virgin Mary. Icons, Marian and otherwise, were purged and replaced, figuratively and literally, with language. In essence, then, the "text" (The Bible specifically, but also other devotional texts) became the replacement for holy images and icons such as the Virgin Mary. It was necessary, then, in destroying these locations for the cultural transference of the model for feminine Christianity (Mary) to provide an alternative for women in particular. This alternative came in the form of an expanded literacy among women in general, and a shift in the kind of textual, devotional, and birth communities women participated in.

While childbirth communities in the middle ages and Renaissance were formed around the fact of procreation, devotional communities in the middle ages would seem to exclude themselves from and work against this act in that they were formed around the pursuit of virginity. In the Reformation period, these devotional and childbirth groups moved closer together as the ideal of virginity was replaced to some degree with the ideal of married chastity. With the possible exception of nuns, most women would either give birth themselves, or assist in the births of their friends or family members. While devotional and textual communities made up of nuns, discussed above, would not technically overlap with childbirth communities, many women who studied or owned devotional texts would have been a part of a birth community as well as a devotional community. Further, we can imagine women might have employed the similar techniques in disseminating knowledge of obstetrics and gynecology as other forms of textual knowledge, as I describe in Chapter One. Female textual communities used "literacies" to interpret, perpetuate, and rebel against the cultural structures that defined women and their relationship to God, men and mothering, through a particular process of dissemination of knowledge, through oral transmission (reading aloud, gossiping, teaching), and through private and public reading. The complexity of the reading process is in part defined by the response of a textual community to the culture through a given text and based on the reader's reading skills and strategy. Bartlett writes that reading "is always a process of negotiation between...the culturally activated text and the culturally activated reader, an interaction structured by the material, social, ideological, and institutional relationships in which both texts and readers are inescapably inscribed" (2–3). Which is to say, no matter how isolated a textual community might seem, there is always circulation, perpetuation, and reconfigurations of the larger culture's ideologies of class, gender, religion, and conduct.

Texts such as the devotional works most commonly owned by women, and gynecological and obstetrical manuals, which are thought to have been owned by women, reflect both the ideology of the culture and to some degree the practice of the "reader." They assume a certain kind of subjection and submission on the part of the female reader, and the female reader also exerts a kind of resistance to that force. Bartlett argues that one way this resistance might happen is through the literacy skills a woman may or may not have. A woman's particular kind of schooling, full, interrupted, or non-existent, would require her to come up with substitute meanings of phrases that confounded her; these readings Bartlett calls "reconstructive readings," which might potentially change a work's meaning significantly.[21]

Introduction

This same hypothesis can be applied to the childbirth community that might be processing information through textual transmission, oral transmission, or both.

Since there is no documented evidence before the late-seventeenth century that a particular woman owned a particular medical or midwifery manual such as *Trotula* or *The Byrth of Mankynde* (even though many appear to be directed, for the most part, to a female audience), we must view potential readership cautiously. It might be helpful to define a territory of literacy that accounts for the dissemination of knowledge beyond simple "ownership" of a text. This area might also include representations of birth, which were commonly found in the *Book of Hours*—the text most often owned by women. The construction of female textual communities in the medieval and early modern gynecological manuals taken up in the next chapter illustrates a potential female readership, one that includes a wide range of literacies. Along with the model presented of female textual and devotional communities, these texts provide an image of how women were thought to disseminate knowledge.

The Reproductive Unconscious in Medieval and Early Modern England

CHAPTER ONE

"I wyl wright of women prevy sekenesse"
Female Textual and Birth Communities and the History of Women's Medical Texts

Medical, scientific, and theological theories and practices related to the male and female reproductive system in the medieval and early modern periods provide a foundation for understanding the construction of the "female" and "male." The paradigms set up by medieval and early modern theorists of medicine and science to describe the nature and function of the male and female reproductive body intertwine with practical physiologic experience and theological discourses on man and woman.[1] In this chapter, I briefly describe the medieval and early modern male-formulated medical philosophies of sexuality as a background for understanding the obstetrical and gynecological manuals that directly addressed reproductive practices and the obstetrical texts generated from female experience. I then give an account of birth rituals as implied by these and other texts. Finally, I look at the interplay between the late medieval and early modern obstetrical and gynecological manuals and the female textual and birth communities that these texts were produced for, examining the role of these texts in the construction and imagining of these same female communities. I interrogate the relationship of these texts to contemporary views of the female body in generation, to the role of the midwife in childbirth and society, and to the ritual of childbirth in its special connection with women's spiritual practices.

MEDIEVAL AND EARLY MODERN MEDICAL VIEWS OF WOMEN

Medieval and early modern medical theory and practice were dominated by the classical tradition; laymen and scholars alike revered the medical philosophies and theories of Galen, Socrates, and Hippocrates.[2] These Greek theories were based on the all-encompassing idea that individuals functioned in the same manner as the universe, were made up of the same components as each other, and were governed by the same planetary influences. This theory was readily appropriated into medieval and early modern Christian tradition, where it could easily be incorporated into the biblical concept of the Creation in which God is all things, and we a part of Him. The main tenet of this Greek theory was that the universe was made up of four basic elements: fire (hot and dry), water (cold and wet), earth (cold and dry), and air (hot and wet). The body was dependent on four corresponding humors: choler or yellow bile, phlegm or mucus, black bile, and blood. Well-being, both physical and spiritual, was attained through a careful balance between them; excessive humors would ideally be purged through sweating, crying, urinating, and defecating. When the body lost its ability to perform these functions naturally, intervention was necessary. Physicians based their diagnoses and treatments on these theories for nearly two thousand years.[3] Aristotle and Galen where joined by a long line of philosophers, such as Isodore of Seville, Vincent of Beauvais, and Thomas Aquinas, who characterized women's bodies as simultaneously the physiologic mirror of and subordinate to men. This notion is clearly seen in visual representations of men's and women's reproductive organs in such illustrations as Vesalius' *Tabulae sex* (1538), as shown in *The Byrth of Mankynde*. In these, and other like representations, the female reproductive organ is a simple inversion of the male one. The neck of the uterus is virtually identical with the penis, the Fallopian tubes with the spermatic ducts, and the ovaries with the testicles (See Figure 1).

While men and women were represented in physiologic similitude, women were nonetheless physical mistakes, imperfect men. Galen advanced Hippocrates' notions about women that theorized that women were colder, wetter, and more phlegmatic than men, and this humoral imbalance, in turn, accounted for women's relative instability, irritability, and inferiority, which reinforced Christian notions of women as derived from biblical accounts of the Creation and the Fall. Further, women, in their constant battle to be "balanced," sought to become more hot and dry, and so needed, it was believed, to engage regularly in sexual intercourse with men. These formulations naturally led to the supposed notion that if a woman only became hot enough, her penis would fall out and she would reach perfection and become a man. However, these notions of the "same sex" theory, as explained in Thomas Laqueur's *Making Sex*, become problematized by a text such as *Trotula*, which shows the impracticality of such an event.[4] For example, there is a description of and a remedy for a prolapsed uterus in *Trotula*.[5] One imagines that a prolapsed uterus might be the closest a woman could come to "turning into a man," and yet it is clear from this document that in the practical world of women, it was not experienced as such.

A modified version of Aristotle's views of the role of women in generation also obtained in medieval and early modern notions of reproduction. He argues that only the male produces seed, and the female is simply the vessel:

> The female always provides the material, the male that which fashions it…if, then, the male stands for the effective and active, and the female

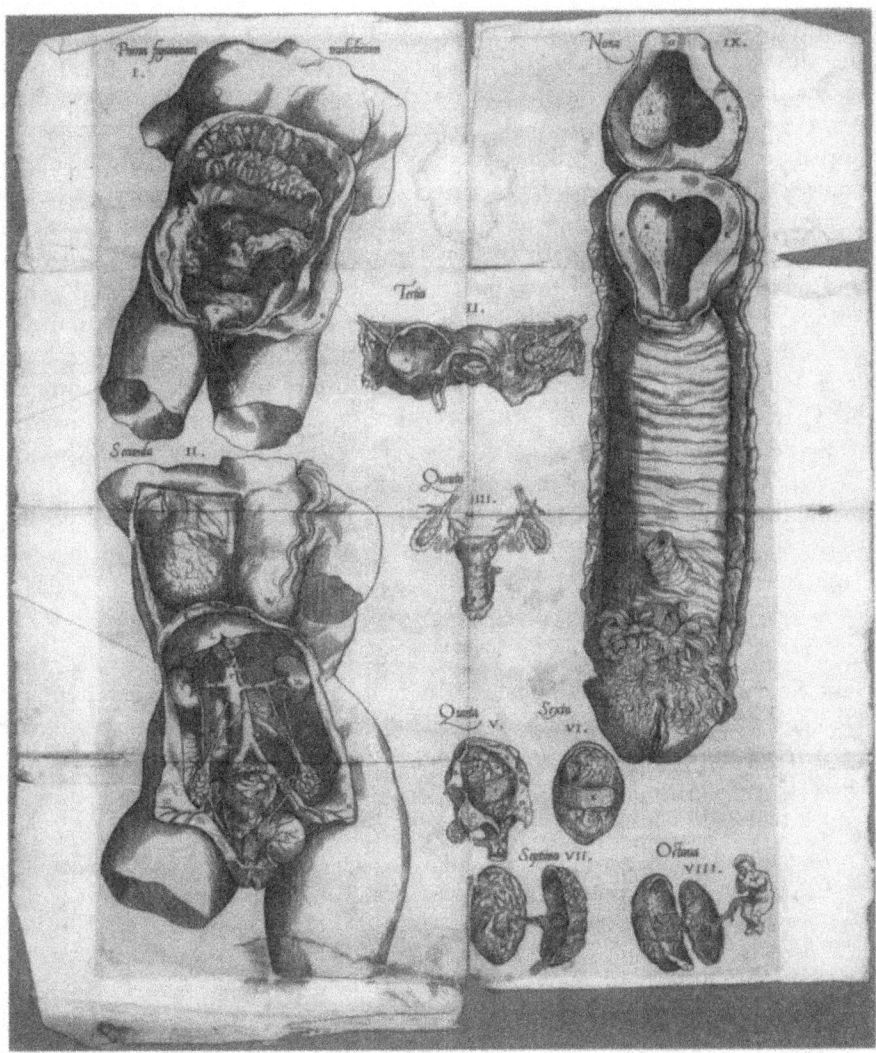

Figure 1. Plate from Thomas Raynald's *The Byrth of Mankynde* (1545) of Vesaulius' 1538 illustrations showing female genitalia and reproductive anatomy. This item is reproduced by permission of *The Huntington Library, San Marino, California*.

considered as female, for the passive, it follows that what the female would contribute to the semen of the male would not be semen but material for the semen to work upon.[6]

While it was generally accepted that women emitted some sort of seed at the time of orgasm, the basic idea that a woman was an empty vessel endured: she provided the matter, the male the seed, or the form. Further, it was argued that in order to conceive a woman had to emit this same seed, and that emission was predicated on her experience of pleasure in intercourse; this, as with the prolapsed uterus, may have been known by women to be, practically speaking, untrue.[7] These ideas were variously taken up and reasserted by theologians such as Jerome, Bonaventure, and Augustine, and were re-instilled into theological discourses and obstetrical and gynecological manuals written by men and women alike.[8] As the female-authored *Trotula* reads: "Therfore ye schal understonde that women have lesse hete in here bodies þan men have and more moistness for defaut of hete þat shuld dryen her moistness & her humors, but netheles of bledyng to make her bodies clene & hoole from syknesse."[9] Even if portions of the *Trotula* text suggest ways in which this text resists certain elements of the medical philosophies structured by men as I have noted above, it still fits to some degree within a framework that casts women as out of balance "imperfections."

BETWEEN WOMEN: RITUALS OF CHILDBIRTH

Jane Sharp was the first English midwife to publish a book on midwifery. Dedicated to Lady Ellenour Talbutt, *The Midwives Book, or the whole art of Midwifery discovered; directing child-bearing women how to behave themselves* was published in London by Simon Miller at the west end of St. Paul's in 1671. The text opens with this statement:

> Sisters,—I have often sate down sad in consideration of the many miseries women endure in the hands of unskilful midwives; many professing they are (without any skill in anatomy, which is the principal part effectually necessary for a midwife) merely for lucre's sake. I have been at great cost in translations for all books, either French, Dutch, or Italian, of the kind. All which I offer with my own experience; humbly begging Almighty God to aid you in this great work; and am your affectionate friend.

This book had at least four editions, and, like its medieval predecessors, the "Sekenesse of Wymmen" and the *Trotula* manuscripts, the prologue motions toward a closed and intimate relationship between the author and her readers. Sharp addresses her potential readers as "Sisters," and refers to herself as the woman's "affectionate friend," always, of course, in the name of God. Her text also includes practical advice on deliveries, including herbal recipes similar to those found in the "Sekenesse" and *Trotula* texts. Unlike its medieval predecessors, however, this text also intimates some anxieties around the practice of "unskillful" midwives akin to those presented in its more immediate early modern predecessors, the *Rose Garden for Pregnant Women and Midwives* and *The Byrth of Mankynde*. Indeed, Sharp suggests that many midwives are ignorant in the very thing that is required of them, and that a text like *Byrth* claims to illuminate: anatomy. Because of the overtly expressed anxieties about midwives and the public nature of *The Midwives Book*, this landmark text marked an end to, rather than a reaffirmation of, the midwife's autonomy and the enclosed female birth space. At this same time, texts by several other men led the way to a veritable burgeoning of books on the subject, paralleling male-midwives and male physicians' entrance into the field.[10]

This bit of Sharp's text is part of what little evidence there is of ritual practices that occurred between women during the "lying-in," or childbirth process. These rituals are important not only to the history of the reproductive female body, but to the development of female textual communities and the transmissions of knowledges between women. This text, even as it heralds the male movement into female domain through physicians and male midwives, shows the residue of an enclosed female space. The cultural performance of these rituals is significant to our knowledge of the development of gendered practices, as well as the dynamics of gossip and female communities.

Just as there are few firsthand accounts by women of the practice of midwifery before the late seventeenth century, there appear to be few accessible historical accounts of the rituals involved in childbirth (the two, of course, being inextricably linked) until well into the seventeenth century. This is perhaps in part because social historians have overlooked the ritual of childbirth, addressing instead only the rites of churching and baptism—events more often documented by a record-keeping institution such as the church. This is also in part because of the dearth of information surrounding the ceremony of birth; after all, birth was a virtually female ritual until well into the seventeenth century, and women were traditionally less often able to write, and therefore less likely to record their experiences. In addition, there is some indication that the ritual of childbirth, like the knowledge of midwives, was meant to be kept from men, as Rösslin's *Rose Garden* and other sources suggest.[11] Even though problematic because of their male authorship and late appearance, the contemporary descriptions published in works such as William Sermon's *The Ladies Companion* (1671), Percival Willughby's 1660 edition of *Observations in Midwifery*,[12] as well as some descriptions of several lying-ins found in *The Diary of Ralph Josselin, 1616-1683*,[13] have been useful in constructing a general paradigm of childbirth rituals for such scholars as Adrian Wilson and David Cressy.[14] These sources, together with midwifery manuals such as *Trotula*, the "Sekenesse of Wymmen," *The Rose Garden*, *The Byrth of Mankynde*, and *The Midwives Book*, I approach with caution when trying to piece together the social practice of childbirth and midwifery. While these texts are invaluable in the rare glimpses they give into perceptions and practices of midwifery and childbirth, they are either written by men (who are alienated from the birth plot in general) or, if written by women (as in the case of the *Trotula* manuscript and the Sharp text), they are often (but not exclusively) entrenched in the patriarchal anxieties of female procreation. Also, the frontispiece of Jane Sharp's book gives a unique display of the full range of the ritual, from birth to baptism.[15] Other immediate sources that also suggest some traces of this elusive ritual include representations of birth in various *Books of Hours*, a kind of text commonly owned by women, and bits and pieces gleaned from diaries, letters, and autobiographies of women throughout late medieval and early modern England.[16] While the fact that these texts reflect a female ritual from a male point of view does not necessarily limit them, it does suggest a view from the "outside." Nevertheless, these are the locations in which there are some traces of the process of childbirth and maternity. I gathered information from other studies of childbirth rituals mentioned above and various midwifery manuals to formulate a paradigm and general framework for the birth ritual, and I apply them to other texts to theorize ways in which the elements and practice of childbirth were negotiated on different levels.

Examining representations and images of birth rituals and subjecting them to political readings, by which I mean readings which expose the ways the rituals express underlying conflict as part of what makes up the "reproductive unconscious," helps us to understand the nature of the conflicts they reveal. One reading of representations of birth and its rituals and the conflicts revealed by these rituals, suggests that men possess agency while the women are passive; women become the objects, rather than the subjects, of reproductive rituals. Another sees these rituals as a competition between men and women, in which women have equal, if not surpassing, agency.[17] Both of these models essentialize the cultural conflict as based on sexual difference, which to some degree it is; men, after all, did not give birth. While sexual difference in part is at the heart of the signification of birth, I want to suggest that certain representations of childbirth rituals complicate our notions about the conflict that existed between the cultural notions and practices of reproduction based on sexual difference. Specifically, images of childbirth show how men and women both struggled with the conflicting doctrines that asked them to be fruitful and also chaste and emerge in particularly arresting ways in devotional texts that seek to teach virginity and enclosure.

A PARADIGM FOR CHILDBIRTH RITUALS

The ritual of birth has some of the characteristics of other significant rites of passage, in that the process involves three phases: separation, transition, and reincorporation.[18] The separation process involves the pregnant woman and her female participants setting themselves apart from men and society—physically, emotionally, and spiritually—using various symbolic and ceremonial gestures. The transition phase includes easing the mother back into the company of those outside her birth circle, including the father and other men, from the lying-in space to the rest of the house. The process is completed with reincorporation through the churching of the mother in the sanctioned location of the church. This is, of course, a general rubric and not an absolute that I am presenting; each stage of the process could vary in minor ways from woman to woman, birth to birth, class to class, age to age. For example, women of the higher classes tended to remain separate from men longer than did women of the lower classes.

SOCIAL SEPARATION

The pregnant woman probably made arrangements for who would attend her birth a good deal before she went into labor (as we do today). As a rule, attendants would include a midwife and several other women, usually ranging in number from five to six or so. These women might include the mother's mother, sisters, mother-in-law, and close friends, but would not, of course, include any men.[19] Also important in the separation, in addition to the exclusion of men, was the collective female activity. The group of women involved in and invited to a birth were known as "gossips."

The etymology of the word *gossip* suggests that a number of different roles were ascribed to the term over a period of many years. The etymology of the word gossip also suggests, in addition to showing a connection between gossip and childbirth, that there was a growing connection of the feminine with gossip (and hence the female body with unbridled speech). The earliest citation of the word gossip in the *Oxford English Dictionary* is as a noun and is dated 1014. It reads: "One who has contracted spiritual affinity with another by acting as a sponsor at a baptism. In relation to the person baptized: a godfather or godmother; a sponsor" (*s.v.* "gossip" n.1). This definition doesn't emphasize the gossip as being a person of one sex more often than the other. In fact, all of the variant definitions refer to both a godmother *and* a godfather. The use of gossip as a noun (1362) is defined as: "a familiar acquaintance, friend, chum. Formerly applied to both sexes, now only to women" (1c). This movement toward associating gossip specifically with women becomes even more acute in the second definition. In the late-sixteenth century, the noun is defined as "Applied to a woman's female friends invited to be present at a birth," and also "A person, mostly a woman, of light and trifling character, esp. one who delights in idle talk" (*s.v.* "gossip" n. 2). These later definitions show explicitly the gossip's role in childbirth and suggest a trend toward emphasizing gossips as women, and associating gossips with trivial and idle character traits and behavior. According to the *OED*, the use of gossip as a verb did not appear until about 1601. The definition reads: "To be a gossip or sponsor to; to give name to" (s.v. "gossip" v.1). A modern use appears (not too long after) in 1627: "To talk idly, mostly about other peoples' affairs" (3). Like the noun, this definition contains similar references to idleness and frivolity—characteristics that appear to be associated with women.

Gossips, then, were involved with the birth process early on as benign godparents who were witnesses to the birth and as godparents at the baptism (which seems to have been attended almost exclusively by women when done in the church). Later on (by definition), gossips performed a number of different tasks and rituals that made up the female birth ceremony (and which carried some anxiety, as the etymology suggests). In addition to gossips attending the birth and making up the female birthing community, there were parties called "gossipings" which took place either before or after the birth in celebration (like a baby shower) of the newly or nearly born, and occurred more often in the upper classes.

Sanctity in Enclosure

The physical space marked out by a female community was as important to the ritual as the social demarcation of space. The idea was to enclose physically the space in order to become removed from ordinary life. Created for the specific purpose of birth, the space was called a "lying-in chamber." The "lying-in chamber" became a kind of womb itself, fully enclosed, and, to some extent, even more impenetrable than the womb it resembled—literally and symbolically. All openings were sealed; windows were closed and covered in order to keep out as much light as possible, and keyholes were also blocked to keep out light. The only source of illumination came from candles. This physical enclosure closely mimicked the enclosed space of anchoresses and anchorites (or vice versa), who lived in a rather small, presumably darkened, room in which their only access to the world was through a small window where they received guests. The special lighting of the candles, and the use of specially made wine (caudle), is also reminiscent of images of church ceremonies. Margaret of Anjou in 1442 makes references to the lying-in chamber in household records. She notes that no men were to enter the lying-in chamber, only "gentlewomen" were allowed to enter for the prescribed period of confinement, up to forty days after birth. She also makes reference to the curtain that was to separate the lying-in space from the living quarters.[20]

This special drink, the caudle, which is hot wine or gruel sweetened with honey or sugar and spices, seems to have been an integral part of the ceremony and was served to the laboring woman by her female assistants in order to help keep up her strength and spirits. In addition to the administering of the caudle, each woman seems to have had her own specific duties in assisting the mother in childbirth. The midwife, above the other women, held a special position: it seems as if she alone was allowed to touch the genitals of the laboring woman. In addition, she had the special job of swaddling the newborn, and, perhaps most significantly, she had the ability to baptize the baby in the case of an emergency.

Timely Transition

Following the event of the birth itself came a lying-in period, which lasted perhaps up to a month, "her month." This period seems to have been divided into three stages, the first of which was confinement in bed (from three days to two weeks in the darkened, womb-like room). During this time, the woman's "privities" were maintained through the application of poultices and bathing in herbs. Her bedclothes were to go unchanged during this period. After this confinement, there was the "upsitting" when linens were changed, and the woman would stay mostly in bed for another week to ten days. After this, the woman could move around the house, but did not go outside for another week or so.[21] During this period, male access to the new mother was limited at first, and then, over the course of the confinement, became more relaxed.[22] At this point she would be reintegrated into society through the sanctified ecclesiastical practice of Purification, or Churching.[23]

Sacred Reintegration (Churching)

Churching was practiced for centuries by both the Catholic Church and later the Reformed Church of England. Catholics originally called this rite "purification." By the year 1552, the reformed church began referring to the ritual as a "thanksgiving" of women after childbirth.[24] The woman traditionally visited the church for this reintegration and purification in the company of the women who attended her birth, including the midwife. The midwife sometimes had the honor of carrying the child. Perhaps as a way of enclosing her symbolically until the ceremony had been performed, the mother would wear a veil in the procession: this was a surviving element of the Catholic purification ritual. Some parishes had a special pew for churching women—variously called an uprising seat, child-bed pew, child-wife pew, or churching pew.[25] Churching is a relatively better known element of the birthing ritual because this event took place in the church, a consistent record-keeping institution, and was more likely to draw the interest of, and be recorded by, church clerics.

The Emergence of Obstetrical and Gynecological Manuals

There is not yet a catalogue of the scientific and medical texts in Middle English although there is one being compiled by Patricia Deery Kurtz and Linda Eshram Voigts), and this section is in no way meant to act as a comprehensive guide to these texts.[26] Rather, this section is intended to act as a general background to the texts commonly referred to as *Trotula*, as well as a few other related works significant to the period.[27] In 1981, Beryl Rowland published *The Medieval Woman's Guide to Health: The First English Gynecological Handbook*. Rowland's transcription of *The Medieval Woman's Guide* has been particularly useful in drawing attention to some of the actual medieval medical obstetrical and gynecological practices of women, and (ostensibly) from a female practitioners point of view. Wendy Arons, in her 1994 English translation of Rösslin's German midwifery treatise *The Rose Garden for Pregnant Women and Midwives* (Der Swangern frawen und he bammen roszgarten)(1513), suggests a changing relationship between men and the reproductive female by locating specific ways in which men began infiltrating women's childbirth practices in Germany.[28] And while Arons has published a modern translation of Rösslin's *The Rose Garden*, there is not as yet a published modern edition of England's most significant midwifery treatise of the mid-sixteenth and mid-seventeenth centuries, Raynald's translation of *De partu hominis*, *The Byrth of Mankynde*. I point in this section to the ways that these texts may have manifested themselves within female textual communities, and how they may have set the stage for the invasion of the male-midwife and physician into women's birth communities. I try here to give a sense of the practical use of medieval obstetrical and gynecological texts, while keeping in mind contemporary views of the female body and its role in childbirth and generation. I do this by first mapping the tradition of the significant vernacular obstetrical and gynecological texts of the medieval period, by trying to reconstruct the texts' audience, and by theorizing a means by which information may have been disseminated among women.

TROTULA AND THE "SEKENESSE OF WYMMEN"

The medieval *Trotula* texts are attributed to an eleventh-century woman named Trotula, who came out of the then-famous medical school of Salerno, Italy. To her are attributed several treatises on the treatment of diseases of women and children, most notably *De passionibus mulierum curandarum*, *De ornat*, *Trotula major*, and *Trotula minor*. There are complications with attributing the *Trotula* manuscripts, both the Latin versions and their Middle English translations, to the work of a woman named Trotula at all. John F. Benton has argued very persuasively that the group of manuscripts that have long been attributed to Trotula may have been written by a woman (although he suspects it was a man or several men), but there is no indication that it was the individual Trotula.[29] Instead he argues that the woman Trotula is more likely the author of a separate text, which can be found in what he calls the Madrid manuscript, and which also appears in the Wroclaw manuscript. The Madrid manuscript contains a medical text which "is an easily portable physician's handbook containing a collection of Salernitian medical texts, including...a Salernitas physician and author whose work also appeared in the Wroclaw manuscript."[30] This text appears to be titled *Practica secundum Trotum*, and later, *Practica secundum Trotulam*. While the treatise begins with gynecological remedies and other advice concerning women and children, the text, Benton argues, is addressed to both men and women. It has a number of chapters in which the medical advice is aimed at both men and women, and in which the patient is referred to as a male, which is divergent from the *Trotula* manuscripts that emerge in the later middle ages. Benton argues that the *Trotula* manuscripts offer more "systematic and fully developed" gynecological information than the *Practica*. He observes that "on the whole, the remedies prescribed in the *Practica secundum Trotam* differ from those in the three texts attributed to Trotula....*Practica*...seems to represent the traditions of empirics and midwives" (43). This statement, while not specifically judging the value of these texts (in fact Benton notes that "academic medicine may even have been more harmful than the empiric practices"), does echo both a modern and contemporary sentiment towards midwives and women practitioners in general, that they are less learned in physiological theories and therefore less capable in practice.[31] Most likely the opposite was the case, since the theoretical and written treatises on women's health and gynecological and obstetrical matters were inevitably removed from the actual practice. The recipes in these manuscripts, for example, could easily be altered through a faulty transcription (such errors in transcription were not uncommon), which could render the recipe either dangerous or useless. Those who were practitioners or midwives and had direct experience with herbal medicine and childbirth would not make the mistakes of those who did not work directly with patients or plants and herbs.

Despite modern skepticism, the idea that a woman named Trotula authored these texts was maintained for several centuries following the appearance of the texts; a number of scribes and authors starting in the thirteenth century refer to her, quote her, and praise her knowledge and ability.[32] I, therefore, operate under the assumption that the texts, if not female authored, were for the most part received as such by contemporaries. Attribution of these texts to a female author may have been initially accepted in the middle ages by male patrons and physicians in part because men, for the most part, knew very little about female physiology. Thus, it would be necessary at some point, perhaps even desirable, to be able to claim through male-formulated texts a kind of direct access to the secrets of women and their sexuality. Take, for example, the popularity of Pseudo-Albertus Magnus late-thirteenth-century *De secretis mulierum*, Eucharius Rösslin's early-sixteenth-century German treatise *The Rose garden for Pregnant Women and Midwives*, and Raynald's mid-sixteenth century *The Byrth of Mankynde*. All these texts, successors to Trotula's *Diseases of Women*, and in several respects inheritors of the information found in texts commonly attributed to Trotula, profess access to and knowledge of women's physiologic secrets. This profession is, as Karma Lochrie argues, "a rhetorical device and primary discursive mode by which culturally transmitted knowledge is authorized and configured."[33] The desire to have access to and manage female physiology is both the source of and the reason for a proliferation of these kinds of texts, especially those quick on the heels of the invention of the printing press.

While Beryl Rowland has transcribed MS Sloane 2463, the basis of her book *Medieval Woman's Guide to Health*, to represent the vernacular obstetrical and gynecological text of *Trotula* available to women in late medieval England, her work does not take into account the multiple obstetrical and gynecological manuscripts extant, and the various audiences to whom they were addressed.[34] So, while Rowland's transcription and translation is a convenient text to consult regarding women's gynecological and health practices, there are some complications involved with reading this text as a translation of the Latin *Trotula*, a fact which makes it more difficult to track accurately potential authorship and readership alike. In her essay "Obstetrical and Gynecological Texts in Middle English," Monica Green gives a descriptive overview of several vernacular obstetrical and gynecological manuscripts and their Latin sources, including those identified as either *Trotula* or the "Sekenesse of Wymmen." As an entry into a discussion of these texts, Green examines the Middle English manuscript source of Rowland's transcription and identifies its Latin source as not primarily the *Trotula* manuscript (as Rowland identifies it), but rather an as yet "inadequately described gynecological text."[35] The "Sekenesse of Wymmen" is a translation of most of the gynecological and obstetrical chapters of Gilbertus Anglicus' *Compendium medicinae* (c.1240), and appears to have circulated in the fifteenth century, and was "far more popular than even the *Trotula* texts."[36] Green also identifies five versions of translations from the Latin *Trotula* manuscripts found in England.[37]

Translation A (translated sometime in the mid-to late-fourteenth century during the reign of Edward III, or early Richard II) appears most "original" in quality, with the greatest number of extended discussions included on female anatomy and physiology of comparative texts. This translation is addressed to women, potentially suggesting a female readership and textual community:

> Wherfor in whochep of ower lady and of all þe seynts I thynke to do myn intent and bessyns for to schew after the french and latyn þe diveris of þe maldis and þe signes þat ye schall know theme by...And þerfor every womann redet vnto oþer þat can not so do and helpe hem and concell theme in her maladis withowt schewyng her desses vnto mann. And if any mann rede þis I charge theme on owor ladys behalf þat he redit not in despyt ner slander of no womann ner for no caus but for þe helpe or hele of them, dredyn þe venjones þat myght fall to theme as hath do to oþer þat hath schewyt þe privyts of þeme in slanderyng of hem. And vnderstend þat þey haue non oþer evellis þat now ben on lyve than þo womenn haden þat now be seyntys in heven.[38]

This passage imagines both a textual and birth community, presuming a mix of women who can and cannot read, while envisioning how knowledge gets transmitted from one group to another: "And þerfore every womann redet vnto oþer þat can not so do and helpe and concell theme in her maladis." This passage also suggests that the women counsel each other, at the same time warning them against allowing male penetration into their community of women. A female community practicing this kind of "counseling" is traditionally portrayed in contemporary texts as a dangerous gathering of women gossips.[39] The fact that the text recommends gossiping as a means of transferring the text suggests female authorship and a female audience and birth community with some degree of literacy. In addition, the author takes great pains to admonish male readers that if they should participate in reading this text they will "dredyn þe venjones þat myght fall to theme as hath do to oþer þat hath schewyt þe privyts of þeme in slanderyng of hem." That is, if they should reveal these "secrets" they will have betrayed "ower lady" and all the saints, and may be punished, presumably by God. A similar and softer sentiment is expressed in Gilbertus Anglicus' text, the "Sekenesse of Wymmen" (the text of which is the basis for Rowland's transcription and translation, but which is different from *Trotula*).[40] Like the prologue to the *Trotula* manuscript, the prologue of this text seems to be addressed to a specifically female readership as well:

> For as moche as ther ben manye women that hauen many diuers maladies and sekenesses nygh to þe deth and thei also ben shamefull to schewen and to tellen her greuaunces vnto eny wyght, therfore I schal sumdele wright to herre maladies remedye, praying God ful of grace to sende me grace truly to write to þe pleasaunce of God & to all womannes helpyng.[41]

While "Sekenesse" expresses women's modesty and reluctance to "tellen her greuaunces vnto eny wyght" (that is, any man), it lacks the more explicit warning of male penetration into a female community of the above version, suggesting a potentially male audience:

> And therfore, in helping of women I wyl wright of women prevy sekenesse the helpyng, and that oon woman may helpe another in her sykenesse & nought diskuern her previtees to such vncurteys men. But neuertheles, whosoeyer he be þat displesith a woman for herr sekeness þat sche hath of þat ordynaunce of God, he doth a gret synne.[42]

This passage, like the one quoted above from Translation A, suggests a female community in which "oon woman may helpe another." It is also imagined as enclosed, so that women may reveal or divulge or "diskuern" her privities and maladies to each other and not "vncurteys men." However, while the man who holds a woman in contempt for her physical situation does "gret synne," he is not overtly threatened with the vengeance of God as he is in Translation A.

"The Sekenesse of Wymmen," Green argues, was likely to have been more widely circulated than those texts translated from the various *Trotula* manuscripts because Version 1 of this text circulated originally in the fifteenth century as a separate, more portable and affordable fascicle or pamphlet. While this suggests a greater likelihood of a wider readership, it is not clear that the readership was necessarily a primarily female one. The text "never addresses the patient herself or the midwife," as some translations of *Trotula* do.[43] In addition, several sections of this version have recipes in Latin, which a lay female audience would be unlikely to understand or to use. It is impossible, however, to argue for a purely male or female, "literate" or illiterate, professional, clerical, or lay readership for any of these texts. Translation C, which is titled the "Boke Mad [by] a Woman Named Rota," is a translation of a few chapters from the *Trotula major* and *Trotula minor* and, like Translation A (*Trotula*), has some material that suggests the text was intended for a patient's practical use, rather than a physician's theoretical use. For example, the author uses on occasion the second person to direct the female patient, and refers to practitioners in very limited terms. The title suggests that the text was authored, scribed, or translated by a woman, yet this title is absent in some other manuscript versions of this text. While a sense of who owned such texts might give some indication of a texts' readership, it is not an inaccurate gauge either.

In fact, other versions of the *Trotula* do not give as clear an indication of female audience as Translation A does, perhaps because their likely audience was clerical. Translation B (the *Liber Trotuli*) and Translation D (*Secreta Mulierum*) show no signs of being intended for women. The *Liber Trotuli* refers to the patient in the third person, while others use second person, and cites Galen and Hippocrates as authors of its cures, as does *Secreta Mulierum*, which claims to be drawn from "þe fadrsly help of epocras and Galyene þe fylosofers and faderys of fysek," but has the same general content as the other texts.[44] It is likely that these texts, which were often bound with other medical and scientific texts in Latin and English, were intended for use by clerics and medical practitioners.

What Women and Their Midwives Really Want: *The Rose Garden for Pregnant Women and Midwives* and *The Byrth of Mankynde*

Because of the printed nature of the German *The Rose Garden for Pregnant Women and Midwives* (1513) and the English translation of this text, *The Byrth of Mankynde* (1540), it is easier to get a sense of both the authorship and intended audience of these works than of their medieval manuscript counterparts. Both texts are arguably the most significant midwifery handbooks of their kind in their respective countries and remained so for many years and through many printings. *Rose Garden* appeared in numerous editions over a period of about eighty years, while *Byrth* was used heavily for about one hundred thirty and years before more updated handbooks became available in the mid-to late-seventeenth century. There are several other midwifery handbooks which were popular during the seventeenth century, including James Guillemeaus' *Child-Birth Or, The Happy Deliverie of*

Women (1612), Jacob Reuff's *The Expert Midwife* (1637), and Jane Sharp's *The Midwives Book: Or the Whole Art of Midwifery Discovered* (1671), but *Rose Garden* and *Byrth* were among the earliest of the early modern texts of this kind, and also the most widely used.⁴⁵ While my project mostly concerns the contents and uses of *The Byrth of Mankynde*, I am interested in how *Rose Garden* spawned and paralleled *Byrth*'s content, and how it took part in undermining female birth communities and, consequently, important textual and social communities as well. Several things clearly happened with the advent of printed texts focused on women's medical needs in the late-fifteenth and early-sixteenth century. The texts take on an instructional, almost corrective tone, they become more clearly addressed to a particular readership (or at least we have more access to information about the readership for whom they were intended), and, I argue, they are actively interested in constructing a fear in women about childbirth, their bodies, and the midwives who attended them.

Eucharius Rösslin's German *The Rose Garden for Pregnant Women and Midwives*, was originally published in 1513 and reprinted fourteen times between 1513 and 1541, and ten times in an expanded version, the *Midwives Booklet*, between 1562 and 1608. The text was translated into Latin (*De partu hominis*) by Rösslin's son in 1532. *Rose Garden* is divided into twelve chapters; the first nine chapters deal with pregnancy and delivery, the last three chapters concern the care, handling and feeding of a newborn. It includes several illustrations of the presentation of the child in utero—all odd and inaccurate in terms of the child's proportions—and an illustration of a birthing chair (Figure 2). These identical figures also appear in *The Byrth of Mankynde*. *Rose Garden*'s popularity and availability, like the later *Byrth*, was in part due to printing technology and the increase in literacy during the Reformation. Also, it is the first clear and public indication that midwives were expected to read, although I suspect that there was some degree of literacy among midwives even earlier than this, based in part on the oaths they were required to take related to baptism regulations.⁴⁶

Like some of its medieval predecessors, *Rose Garden* addresses in its prologue a specifically female readership, that of pregnant women and midwives. Unlike its predecessors, however, the discourse clearly comes from a position of anxiety as is illustrated in part by the tone and composition of the text's dedication, prefatory poem and prologue. Rösslin, in his dedication to "the illustrious highborn princess and lady Katherine," follows the traditional trope of humbling himself to his patron. Yet he also positions himself not just as the bearer of information, but as a mediator of sins and an agent of redemption. This mechanism of coupling the obsequious with the patronizing, and the administrator of knowledge with the redemptor, signals Rösslin's own complicated position relative to the pregnant woman and her deliverer:

> I...offer my humble obedient willing service....I find in the third chapter of the book of creation That the almighty eternal God punished our very first

mother Eve for violating the commandment with the curse that she should bear her children in pain...and although this pain may not be completely abolished or hindered by any reason wisdom or art yet if pregnant women behave themselves properly before and during birth...then such pain may be tempered or lessened....I am ready and willing out of humble and obedient duty to Y.R.H. to publish everything that it is necessary for the pregnant bearing woman and midwife to know.[47]

The notion that a man could know "everything that it is necessary" for a woman to know about her own body, and a midwife to know about her own practice (from which men like Rösslin were, for the most part, excluded) may have seemed strange to women who had traditionally put their obstetrical and gynecological care in the hands of midwives and other female practioners.

Texts like *Rose Garden* and *Byrth* were dedicated to aiding pregnant women and their midwives in the birth process, but these texts also created a current of suspicion. Clearly, on the one hand, Rösslin's purpose is genuinely to support women and their midwives by supplying them with vital information. And yet the fervor with which Rösslin warns the pregnant woman about the danger of ill-trained midwives, particularly in the prefatory poem, "Admonition to Pregnant Women and Midwives," no doubt caused suspicion and anxiety among women reading this text. Rösslin plants this suspicion and anxiety through a series of strategic devices which situates men as having the power (along with God) to save the souls of children, as having the knowledge to inform women about their bodies and the proper behavior for a good delivery, and as having the wisdom of knowing how to handle and disseminate information. He opens the poem by suggesting that men occupy a privileged position in relation to God:

> How very close to man God is
> ...His creation's comfort to obtain
> And this he earned with such great pain
> That he redeemed it with his own blood
> as any father's done
> Who tears apart both body and land
> At seeing his child in danger's hands.[48]

He suggests that, like Christ, man sacrifices himself to save his children from the negligent and evil midwife:

> ...In thought and feeling I contend
> That we must work without an end
> Whene'er a newborn's brought to light
> To save its soul with all our might
> ...For what God gives us with such care
> That we destroy it totally
> And such great things go unperceived
> I mean the midwives each and all

> Who know so little of their call
> That through neglect and oversight
> They destroy children far and wide
> And work such evil industry
> That they take life while doing their duty
> And earn from this a handsome fee.[49]

Rösslin suggests that "each and all" midwives are negligent and incapable of caring for the souls of the young, and, worst of all, they accept money for this "evil industry"—supposedly a lot of money. He successfully creates a multi-level anxiety about a child's physical and spiritual self, while suggesting the male physician's desire to take over this seemingly lucrative industry (in fact, midwives generally, with the exception of some royal midwives, didn't make much money).[50]

Rösslin ends his poem by appropriating the midwife's position while trying to elide the difference between theory (official medical education) and practice. At the same time he sets up a dichotomy between that which women do with their art, and that which men do—and how they do it:

> ...Midwives'll find their art here written
> I've given them what they must know
> Which they have in this small quarto
> In it they'll find good report
> Of what happens in human birth
> ...And since no midwife that I've asked
> Could tell me anything of her task
> I'm left to my medical education
> Which takes such things in consideration
> I've put it down quite pleasantly
> In honor of feminine courtesy
> This must be understood verily
> So women do not feel ashamed.[51]

Rösslin claims to have written the art of midwifery, which can be bought and owned by anyone, exploiting the secrets of what he calls human birth. His method of disseminating knowledge is the preferred (male) form: good report, and, significantly, publication and widespread marketing. The alternative is something that he is, like midwifery and birth itself, excluded from: female gossip. He admits in the passage that "no midwife...could tell me anything of her task," thus leaving him to theoretical, not practical, models. Although he suggests in his phrasing and tone that midwives were incapable of articulating their practice, requiring them to write their guidelines for them, one can also read his assertion as a reluctance on the part of the midwives to reveal the secrets of their trade and risk male intrusion into a sacred female space.[52]

Rösslin's 1512 German handbook found an ample and prosperous market in England, as well as other European countries. Translated in England as the *Byrth of Mankynde*, the earliest edition (1540) cites Richard Jonas as the translator of the Latin *De partu hominis*, printed by "T.R." (Thomas Raynald, a printer of the era).[53] Later editions are uniformly attributed to Thomas Raynald, Physician, and seem to make no mention of either Jonas, *De partu hominis*, nor Rösslin, although there is a reference which must be to Jonas in the Prologue of at least the 1545 and 1552 editions.[54] In addition, later versions are different in several respects from the earliest edition, including the addition of anatomical illustrations of particular interest in the 1545 and 1560 editions (Figure 1).[55] While the text is specifically designed for and addressed to a primarily female audience, it should be noted that the only evidence so far (at least) that a woman owned a copy of *Byrth* exists thanks to an inscription found in a 1626 edition: "1681, Mary Buxton owns this Book." There is as yet no concrete evidence of like nature that a woman owned a copy of either the *Trotula* or "Sekenesse" manuscripts.[56]

The numerous editions of *The Byrth of Mankynde* suggest an increasing number of literate men and women interested in the knowledge provided by a text like *Byrth*. Its wide availability also suggests an increasing participation of men in obstetrical and gynecological care of women. *Byrth*, like *Rose Garden*, was clearly designed as a handbook, but it also does other kinds of work relative to the culture's relationship to the notion and activity of childbirth and its rituals. The author suggests that the texts can act as a kind of intermediary (and a male one at that) between the exclusive practice of midwives and the scientific theories of men. *Rose Garden* and *Byrth* act as "male" intermediaries between the laboring mother and midwife, ultimately opening up a formerly female domain to male physicians and male-midwives, while also publicly marketing the secrets of women. The end result is, in fact, not just the infiltration of the *business* of midwives and midwifery, but a penetration into the nearly sanctified ceremony of childbirth itself by these male-midwives and physicians.[57]

The Byrth of Mankynde ran through what appears to be a total of thirteen editions, appearing in England in 1540, 1545, 1552, 1560, 1564, 1565, 1598, 1604, 1613, 1626, 1634, 1654, and 1676.[58] I will briefly outline the general composition of the texts, with particular attention to the nature of the 1540 edition, which contains a unique six-page dedication to "the most gracious and in all goodnesse most excellent vertuous Lady Quene Katheryne," as well as the prologues and contents, when applicable, of the 1545, 1560, and 1565 editions.[59] All of the editions of *Byrth* after the 1540 edition have the same general layout: they are divided into four books concerning conception, pregnancy, and infant care. The first book generally concerns pregnancy and the care of the mother's body, the second deals with presentations in childbirth and delivery techniques and difficulties (including delivering a dead fetus from a live mother, and a live fetus from a dead mother), the third book largely deals with the care and feeding of infants and children's diseases, and the fourth book addresses issues

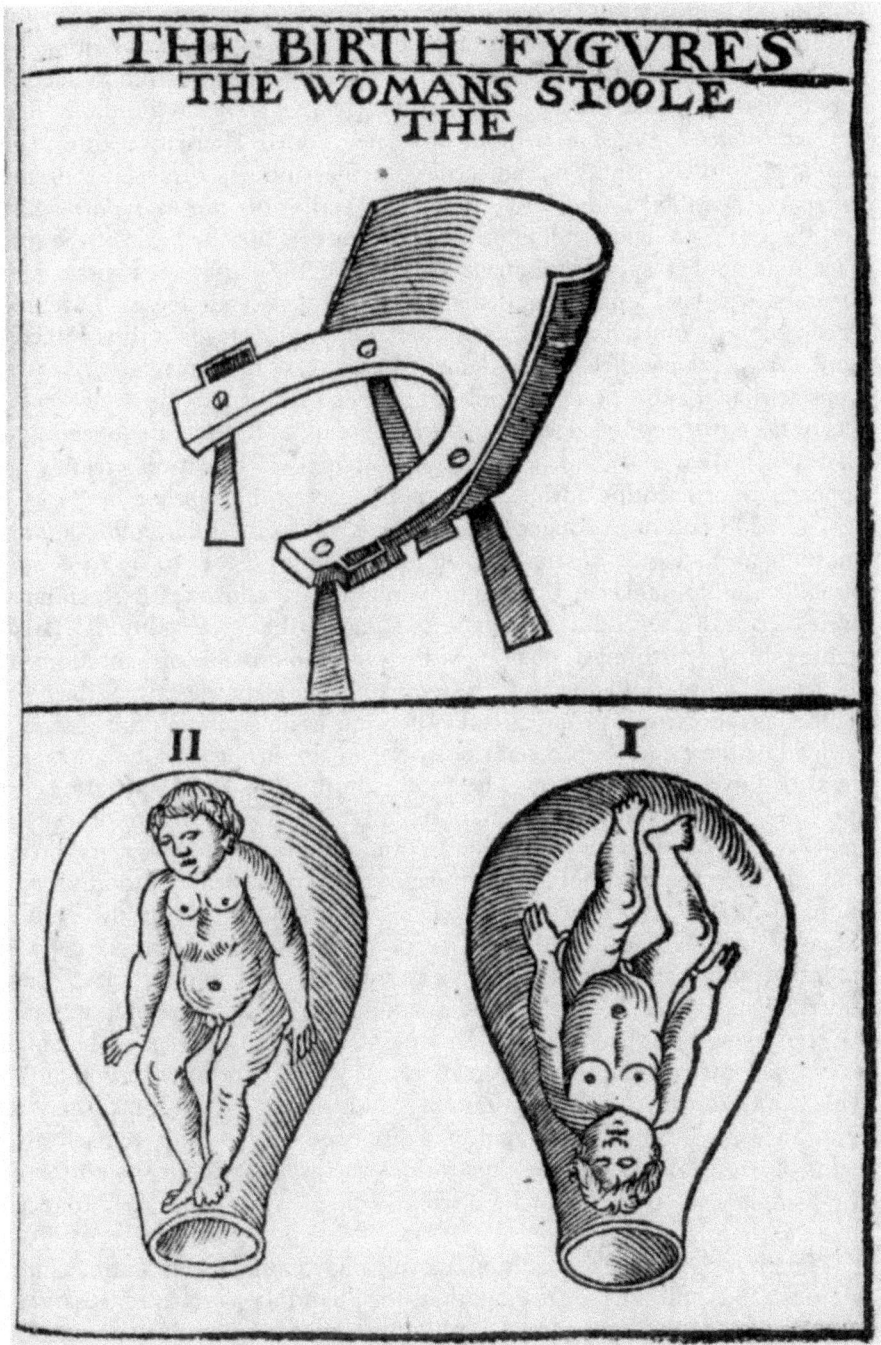

Figure 2. Illustrations from *The Byrth of Mankynde* (1560) showing birthing stool and fetal positions. This item is reproduced by permission of *The Huntington Library*, San Marino, California.

of cosmetics and sterility. None of these books deals directly with the ritual surrounding childbirth because men did not participate in this ritual.

The 1540 edition of *Byrth* is the most markedly different from its successors in that its title is simply *The Byrth of Mankynde, newly tranlsated out of Latin into Englysshe*, without the later added alternative title, *The Womans Booke*. There is no indication of either author or translator on the title page (possibly an indication of deferred authority), nor in the prologue, and there is a "religious admonition to the reader" on the back of the title page that doesn't appear in later editions. The 1540 *Byrth* is divided into three books (later editions are divided into four), and doesn't have the "Prologue to Women Readers" as the later editions do (save for the 1660 edition). This text parallels the "original" Latin version from which *Byrth* is translated, in that the first two books of *Byrth* correspond to the twelve chapters of *De partu hominis*. However, the third book of *Byrth* both appears and claims to be new and "independent" or "original" information, creating an appearance of scientific advancement on the part of the "author."

The 1545 edition is longer, about 170 leaves in the folio, and contains anatomical plates (of Vesalius) not found in either the 1540 or 1565 editions. It also contains the birth figures found in Rösslin's text, which have been identically reproduced in at least some of the *Byrth* editions. These figures show a birthing stool along with seventeen possible presentations of the fetus (Figure 2). In all cases, the fetus (or fetuses, in the case of the twin figures) is represented proportionally the same as an adult and fully extended (rather than curled in a fetal position) in the uterus; these figures are described in the first chapters. The 1552 edition is similar in appearance to the 1545 edition, but includes marginalia which shows a figure of a pregnant woman or midwife with extended and overstated index fingers, probably indexing the text, but also echoing examination form. In addition, the more accurately represented anatomical plates show the uterus with a fetus, as well as a dissected male torso. Further, the plates represent the Fallopian tubes and vaginal canal as an internal penis and testicles. These illustrations are also described and are followed by this revealing remark: "Here ye shal be aduertysed that although these two fyrst fygures be made principally for ye man, yet may they serue as wel to express the woman."[60] This quotation reveals a long-standing tradition of the elision of and an ignorance regarding female anatomy discussed above. This remark also helps buttress, along with the illustrations themselves, Laqueur's notion of the "single sex" theory that he attributes to medieval and early modern medical theorists.[61]

The Preface to the 1545 edition, interestingly enough, is in Latin, as it is in the 1552 edition, suggesting that this handbook wasn't necessarily intended solely for lay women. Rather, it is addressed to those learned in Latin and perhaps interested in more theoretical works, as well as for "simple" women. Raynald translates the Preface following the Latin in the later 1552 edition:

> Albeit some Aristarchus may perhappes finde some lacke of faithfulness and diligence in this work: yet there is none so froward to deny but that there is some fruit and profyte to bee founde therein, seyng that it commeth nowe abrode much more enlarged and encreased, and more diligently corrected then it was before, eyther in the Latine or in the Englyshe. And where before in the other printes, there lacked matter necessary to the openyng and declaration of the figures pertaynyng to the inner partes: it is nowe so plainely set forrth, that the simplest Mydwyfe which can reade, maye both understand for her better instruction, and also other women that have nede of her be receaved and practysed of Mydwyves and all other Matrones, with no lesse successe, then it is with good wyll and desyre wrytten to profite and to do good to other."[62]

His statement that any simple midwife who can read can access this work either suggests a fair number of literate women, or an audience that may be different than the text purports. In addition to this, Raynald, under the auspices of "good will and desire written to profit and do good" for women and their ignorant midwives, defends the quality of his work. He does this through the use and appropriation of childbirth metaphors. In so doing, he reveals an interest in marketing for financial profit the secrets of reproduction. Raynald also makes it clear that his text is designed even for the "simple" midwife who can read.

In its metaphoric construction, this passage, like the text itself, both aligns itself with and against women. Raynald argues that within his text there is to be found both "fruit" as in useful information and as a metaphor for a fetus, "fruit of the womb," and "profit," as in the benefits from the useful information, as well as the profit gained from marketing the text. The description of the manual as "more enlarged and increased" than previous versions in Latin or English, replicates the pregnant belly it aims to dissect. The fact that he cites the texts as originating "from abroad" also suggests an element of the foreign and unknown, like the mysterious female body itself. Further, continuing with images of conception theory, Raynald writes that previous texts "lacked the matter" necessary to explicate women through the "opening and declaration" of their internal parts. In the theories of conception, as noted above, the male contributed the form, while the female contributed the matter. Therefore, Raynald both feminizes and masculinizes his work: it contains both the matter and the form. Further, he claims that other manuals are unable to "open" and declare women's parts and are therefore not privy to the process of procreation as his text is.

What *Rose Garden* and *Byrth* share, besides material, is a similar tone, not just in the body of the texts, but in the dedications and prologues as well. In his Prologue, Raynald describes the history and process of his translation of *De partu hominis*. He describes the text in terms of its market benefits and the process of translation using images and metaphors of pregnancy and birth as he does in the Preface. Translation, then, becomes like the process of birth itself:

> Wherefore I resolving & earnestly revising from top to[63] the sayde book, and herewithall consyderyng the manifolde utilite & profyte... thoughte my labour and paynes shoulde not be evell employed, ne unthankefully accepid and receauid of all honest, discrete, and sage wemen.[64]

Raynald not only expresses his work as "labour and paynes," but he also sets up the paradigm of a well-controlled, contained, and proper birth, ostensibly attainable through the use of this manual by "honest, discrete and sage" women. The idea of "profit" and use resonates throughout a good portion of the Prologue (in which Raynald frequently threatens to "come to oure pupose," but never actually does), as does his insistence on his superior knowledge of the female body and its privities:

> And farther haue in the fyrst booke let furth and euidently declarid, all the in ward partes of woman (such as were necessary to be knowed to our pourpose) and that not onely in wurdes, but also in lyuely and expresse figures, by the which euery parte before in the describeyd, maye in maner be as exactly & clearely perceauid, as thoughe ye were present at the cuttynge open or anathomye of a ded woman.[65]

Raynald implies here that he has access to all parts of the woman, but is revealing only what is "necessary...to our pourpose." In addition, his knowledge is disseminated, he claims, through lively and expressive figures—suggesting that figures of a "ded" woman are not only illuminating to the process of birth, but are lively examples of women's anatomy and so almost conflating the dead with the quick. Raynald suggests that the only way to understand birth is through anatomy and dissection, yet uses illustrations of a dissection as a substitute for direct access to a woman's experience of birth. But because the practice of birth eludes him, the illustrations that represent the dissection of the dead woman and the fetus within her womb are his closest experience with the practice of the art of childbirth, an experience that he argues is superior to that of midwives.

Perhaps one of the most interesting passages of Raynald's Prologue comes after his description of the contents of the four books in his manual. This passage practices some of the same techniques of its German predecessor. It raises the issue of the competence of midwives, albeit in a softer manner, and succeeds in forcing itself into the circle of women—into a female textual community as well as a female birth community:

> Briefly I require all readers herof to interpretate and construe euery thynge herein contaynyd according to the best: and to use euery thyng therin entreated of, to the pourpose wherfore it was written: for truly as for my parte consyderynge the manyfolde, dayly and imminent daungeours and parells, the whiche all maner of women of what estate, or degre so euer they be, in theyr labours do sustayne and abyde, yea many tymes with parell of theyr lyfe (of which there be so many examples neadelesse here to be rehersed)...Yf by my paynes this lytell treatyse were made to speake Englysshe, as it hath ben long sith tought to speke dutche, frenche,

spanissh, and dyuers other langages: In the which coutries there be few wemen that can reade, but they wyll haue one of these bookes always in redinesse: where also this and other such bookes be as communely solde at euery stacionars shop, as any other boke. The same commodite then and proffet which they in theyr regions do obtayne by enioyinge of the lytell booke in theyr maternal langage, may also ensue unto all women in this noble reaulme of England it beinge lyke wyse sette furthe in oure Englysshe speche: soo that to them whiche diligently wyll aduert, & geue hede to the instructions of this lytell booke, it may supply the roome and place of a goud mydwyfe: & aduise them many tymes of sundry cases, chaunses, and remedies, wherin peraduenture right wise wemen and goud mydwifes shalbe full ignorant...by the occasyon of this booke to frequent & haunt wemen in theyr labours, carienge with them this booke in theyr handes, and causyge suche part of it as doth cheifly concerne the same pourpose, to be red before the mydwife, and the rest of the wemen beyng present.[66]

I quote this passage at length because of the way in which it imagines the childbirth scene with the text as the central figure, and not the laboring woman, midwife, or attending women. Further, in this passage Raynald suggests that the dangers of birth, whether the woman be of high or low estate, can be assuaged by following and properly interpreting his book. In fact, he even goes so far as to imagine several female communities to which this text is addressed—women in "other regions" reading this book in their "maternal" tongue, suggesting an English readership, and women in England during their labors. At the same time Raynald imagines female birth and textual communities reading his book, he seeks to obliterate these same communities. The instructions in this book, he writes, may take the place of a midwife, for his book advises women of things about which the "goud" midwife might be ignorant. In later editions, Raynald warns that "mydwyues, moued eyther of enuye, or els of malice, or both; diligented and endeuoured them very earneslty, by all wayes possible, to finde the meanse to suppresse and abrogate the same, makynge al women of their acquaintaunce...to beleue that it was nothynge worth."[67] By suggesting that midwives are incompetent, and by creating a fear in women that these same midwives tried to suppress this very "honest" text, Raynald attenuates an already existing anxiety about the event of childbirth, thus making a "roome and place" for the male presence and voice in an otherwise exclusive female location.

While *Trotula*, the "Sekenesse of Wymmen," *Rose Garden*, and *Byrth* sometimes give a very explicit sense about their intended audience, there is little indication of what kinds of female rituals really occurred during the birth process. The descriptions of the birth process are prescriptive rather than descriptive, addressing how to handle the physical challenges of removing babies from uteruses, rather than the emotional needs or ritual elements of childbirth. To find the elements of childbirth rituals in the medieval and early modern period, one must look in other and multiple locations, none of which give a singular clear picture of the rituals.

The obstetrical and gynecological manuals of the period draw our attention to the social management of "women's privy sickness" and childbirth, illustrating the ways that women taught and were taught to manage childbirth. The later instructional manuals suggest how men began to take over this field, and how men and women's anxieties about childbirth to some degree fueled this shift. These texts, through the course of their management of childbirth practices, quite naturally engage in imagining and defining the female (birth) communities they address. While we cannot know whether these descriptions are representative of those who actually acquired and used these texts, they imply a particular readership. It seems likely, however, that the commonly known *Trotula* and the multi-edition *Byrth*, along with several other texts, made it into the hands of many an individual desirous of discovering the "secrets" of their birth and eager to allay their fears of their own impending birth experiences. The works that I take up in the following chapters, the *Ancrene Wisse, Hali Meidenhad*, Julian of Norwich's *Book of Showings*, Margery Kempe's *The Book of Margery Kempe*, and Thomas Bentley's *The Monument of Matrones*, engage in a level of dialogue with these instructional manuals. The medieval devotional texts use images of childbirth and its rituals, along with images of female communities, to describe in metaphoric terms spiritual states and insights, while the early modern texts invert this relationship, using sacred images to allay modern fears of women in labor.

CHAPTER TWO
Theologized Maternity in Julian of Norwich's *Book of Showings*

In Chapter 17 of *The Book of Margery Kempe*, Christ instructs Margery, who was "newly delivered of a child," to leave off bearing children and go to Norwich to show the vicar there her privities and the counsel such as Christ shows to her. During this trip, Christ also bids her to go and visit the anchoress "Dame Jelyn." In her visit to Julian, Margery has "many wondirful revelacyons whech sche schewyd to the ankres to wetyn yf ther wer any deceyte in hem for the ankres was expert in swech thyngys and good cownsel cowd gevyn."[1] After Julian gives a speech confirming that Margery's revelations originate from the marvelous goodness of our Lord, and after she instructs Margery in the practice of chastity, it is observed that "mych was the holy dalyawns that the ankres and this creatur haddyn be comownyng in the lofe of owyr Lord Jhesu Crist."[2] These two women spend many days together discussing their holy love of Christ and, as the use of the word "dalyawns" suggests, their encounter and conversation is a spiritual one. However, to see this description of Margery and Julian's encounter as simply "spiritual" is to overlook the multiple nuances of the word "dalyawns."[3] The *Oxford English Dictionary* defines the word as "talk, confabulation, converse, chat; usually of light or familiar kind, but also used of serious conversation or discussion" ("dalliance"1). Certainly one could apply the "serious conversation or discussion" to Julian and Margery's encounter. But one could also read their dalliance in a "lighter" or even a dangerous way, such as a "sport, play, esp. toying or caressing, flirtation; often in a bad sense, wanton toying" ("dalliance"2). This definition implies that the dalliance could be sexual or salacious. Thus, in these various interpretations of this single word does the conflict appear between the sacred, spiritual, and enclosed, converge with the profane, sexual, and worldly.

I begin this chapter on Julian of Norwich with Margery's visit because this dalliance is the hinge that joins these two women who are generally seen to be divergent in their spiritual practices: Margery seeks her spiritual satisfaction through worldly travel, outward sobbing, and a struggle to remain celibate, while Julian seeks her spiritual gratification through the anchoritic practice of enclosure, where she is removed from the world as well as its profane temptations, such as sex and gossip. Margery expresses her spirituality using images of the body, specifically bodily images and metaphors of childbirth and maternity. In her *Book of Showings*, Julian expresses her spirituality through images of God and Christ's maternity.[4] But more importantly, the nuances of this dalliance point to the conflict between the chaste and procreative body and the doctrines that asked men and women especially to be fruitful and multiply and at the same time chaste. This conflict was negotiated on a social level through two kinds of manuals, those instructing women in childbirth practices, such as in the case of the medieval *Trotula* and "Sekenese of wommen," and those instructing women in virginity and enclosure, such as in the case of *Hali Meidenhad* ("A Letter on Virginity") and the *Ancrene Wisse* ("Guide for Anchoresses"). *Hali Meidenhad* argues strongly for female virginity by invoking the horrors of childbirth, and the *Ancrene Wisse* guides women in the everyday practices involved in enclosure. These two texts explain the terms of the conflict between discourses of virginity and maternity that occupy Julian of Norwich in her *Showings*. The conflict made evident by these early medieval texts has implications for Julian's anchoritic practice, suggesting that Julian of Norwich's maternal figurations of God and Christ come out of repressions and distortions of childbirth and are a means by which she attempts to resolve her social experience of maternity with that of the life of enclosure. In this text, Julian works against the notion of women's bodily procreativity and very firmly within the discourse of enclosure—expressing a set of cultural desires which seeks to vanquish women's procreative bodies through the literal enclosure of anchoritic practice or through symbolic enclosure of virginity alone. Thus her text, partially through its occlusion of female procreation and communities, engages in the formation of one feminine subjectivity available in late medieval England.

Our view of these constructions, however, is complicated by the production of the text itself. Existing editions of Julian's *Showings* suggest that there may be scribal fissures that occur in the period of the text's physical production that allow for the possibility of access to the culture's uneasiness concerning images of childbirth in devotional texts. The three existing manuscripts of Julian's full text are from no earlier than the seventeenth century, and they are to a large degree modernized.[5] The erasing or "smoothing over" of many of the traces of Julian's original language makes it difficult to speculate about Julian's own dialect. But, lapses into more archaic or obsolete usage, when they do occur in these modernized texts, may signal the seventeenth-century scribes' own difficult relationship to the language and content of Julian's text. As a result, the relationship of Julian to the images she constructs in her text and the relationship of the seventeenth-century scribes to the language of these images allow us a place to view the reproductive unconscious at work in at least two cultural and temporal locations.

For modern literary critics, the idea that medieval religious women were in part defined or demarcated by their bodily experience is by now accepted. Because of the works of scholars such as Carolyn Walker Bynum, Karma Lochrie, Sarah Beckwith, and Elizabeth Robertson, we understand that medieval notions of the body are indeed quite complex.[6] In her essay "Medieval Medical Views of Women and Female Spirituality in the *Ancrene Wisse* and Julian of Norwich's *Showings*," Elizabeth Robertson draws on medieval medical notions of the female body, in specific on humoral theory, and on contemporary ideas about the female mystic's relationship to Christ's body to argue that "medical ideology shapes the literary representation of the feminine in mystical works."[7] Drawing from Robertson and other works on medical views of women, I look at the way medieval notions of the female reproductive body and anxieties about that body surface in devotional texts intended for women, and I suggest that men's and women's understanding, experience, and anxiety about the chaste and reproductive body shapes literary representations of that body.

HALI MEIDENHAD AND ANCRENE WISSE

Hali Meidenhad and *Ancrene Wisse* are two of the few known surviving English language texts of the early Norman period; they are made more significant by the fact that they were intended for a female audience. The *Ancrene Wisse* was explicitly directed in 1215 to three anchoresses in Deerford near Wigmore Abbey in Herefordshire.[8] These texts, as Elizabeth Robertson has shown us, are significant in that they are crucial to "the proper appreciation of the ways in which audiences untrained in Latin shaped the development of early Middle English Literature."[9] They also imply the existence of a common female audience, and, being male-authored, are "controlled by male assumptions about both the material and conceptual nature of female religious experience," with imagery selected accordingly.[10] In addition to the male assumptions of the nature of the female religious experience, these texts supply the notions of the role of the female within a Christian framework. Whatever these texts indicate about female literacy, their existence suggests that women needed, or at least that men wanted them to have, a literature that delineated their relationship to God in everyday spiritual and anchoritic experience.[11] These texts not only describe the important role of virginity to the maiden's and anchoresses' experience, but they also enumerate the various temptations that face the young woman and anchoress alike, including the possibility of marriage and children. Further, the content of these texts helps to explain the terms of the conflict between discourses of virginity and maternity.

Hali Meidenhad answers to the edict to be fruitful and multiply by describing in painful detail the potential difficulties of marriage and particularly maternity, and by placing the culture's desires for these things with the earthly family rather than the heavenly one. The text begins in Latin: "Audi, filia, et vide, et inclina aurem tuam; et obliuiscere populum tuum et domum patris tui," and then translates into the vernacular (in the words of David the psalmist), "Iher me, dohter, bihald ant beiþ þin eare; ant foȝet ti folc ant tines feader hus"[12] (Hear me, daughter, behold and bend your ear; and forget your people and your father's house).[13] By casting aside the earthly family and by elevating the holy family, the author creates a safe location for the young woman to locate herself outside worldly desires. He continues to turn back and forth from the worldly to the heavenly and what they each provide for a woman. Conventionally, heaven provides a husband in Christ and a father in God. Instead of children, virginity is the "heh dignete" (high dignity) in the face of the Devil. In fact, carnal desire is itself described in terms of parenting: "Avre licomes lust is þes feondes foster" (our physical lust is the fiend's offspring). But it is marriage and childbirth itself that provide the most poignant displays of anxiety provocation, as well as one of the earliest and most detailed, even if not always accurate, descriptions of maternity in English.

The author of *Hali Meidenhad* makes it clear that of the three states, virginity, widowhood, and marriage, marriage is the lowest, even as it is rewarded and "tolerated" in heaven. He then goes on, "as we ear biheten" (as we promised before), to describe in great detail the depths to which a woman drops if she marries and is in servitude to man: "Nu þu art iweddet, ant of se heh se lahe iliht...into flesches fulde, into beastes liflade, into monnes þeowdom, ant into worldes weane."[14] (Now you are married, and from so high [a place] so low alighted, into fleshly filth, into the life of a beast, into man's servitude, and into the world's sorrow). While marriage, according to *Meidenhad*'s author, is rewarded in heaven thirty-fold (as opposed to harlotry or adultery), it is still equated here with succumbing to the lowest earthly place, "fleshly filth" and the "world's sorrow."

Falling into this fleshly filth naturally leads into a discussion of childbearing, and the author illustrates the quandary in which women found themselves in relation to procreative duties:

> Ȝef ha ne mei nawt temen, ha is icleopet gealde; hire lauerd luued hire ant wurdged þe leasse, ant heo, as þeo þet wurst is þrof, biweped hire wurdes.... An nu iwurde hit al þet ha habbe hire wil of streon þet ha wilned...I þe burderne þrof is heuinesse ant heard sar eauer umbe stunde; in his iborenesse, alre stiche strengest, and dead oðerwhiles; in his fostrunge ford, moni earm-hwile.[15]

Theologized Maternity in Julian of Norwich's Book of Showings

(If she may not bring forth [children], she is called barren; her lord loves her and respects her less, and she, as the one that is the worst from it, weeps at her fate...and now should it happen that she have her will of offspring that she desired. In the carrying there is heaviness and hard pain at every hour; in the birthing, the strongest of all pains, and sometimes death; in the nourishing forth, many miserable times.)

If the woman doesn't bear children, she is thought by her peers to be barren and not as well loved by the Lord as those who do bear children. However, the author does not dwell on the edict that creates this anxiety over barrenness (that we be fruitful and multiply). Rather, he suggests that if women do get what they want and bear children they are not esteemed in the eyes of the Lord, but rather are subject to physical pain and suffering:

Ga we nu forde, ant loki we hwuch wunne arised þrefter I burþerne of bearn...þi rudie neb schal leanin, ant ase gres genin; þine ehnen schule doskin, and underneode wonnin, ant of þi breines turnunge þin heaued aken sare. Inwid i ti wombe, swel in þi butte þe bered te ford as a weaterbulge, þine þearmes þralunge ant stiches i þi lonke, ant i þi lendene sar eche riue; heuinesse in euch lim; þine breosetes burþerne o þine twa pappes, ant te milc-strunden þe þerof stirked. þi mud is bitter, ant walh al þet tu cheowest; ant hwet mete se þi mahe hokerliche underued—þet is wid unlust —warped hit eft ut. Inwid al þi wole ant ti weres wunne, fowurdest a wrecche. þe cares ᴈein þi pinunge þrahen bineomed þe nahtes slepes. Hwen hit þenne þerto kimed, þet sore sorhfule angoise, þet stronge ant stikinde stiche, þet unroles uuel, þet pine ouer pine, þet wondrinde ᴈeomerunge; whilt þu swenchest terwid, ant þine deades dute, scheome teke þet sar wid þe alde wifes scheome creft þe cunnen of þet was-sid, hwas help þe biholued, ne beo hit neauer se uncumelich; ant nede most hit þolien þet te þerin itimed.¹⁶

(Let us now go further, and see what happiness comes to you afterwards during pregnancy... Your rosy face will grow thin, and turn green as grass; your eyes will grow dull, and shadowed underneath, and because of your dizziness your head will ache cruelly. Inside, in your belly, a swelling in your womb which bulges you out like a water-skin, discomfort in your bowels and stitches in your side, and often painful backache; heaviness in every limb; the dragging weight of your two breasts, and the streams of milk that run from them. There is a bitter taste in your mouth, and everything that you eat makes you feel sick; and whatever food your stomach disdainfully receives—that is, with distaste—it throws it up again. In the midst of all your happiness and your husband's delight, you are reduced to a wretch. Worry about your labor pains keeps you awake at night. Then when it comes to it, that cruel distressing anguish, that fierce stabbing pain, that incessant misery, that torment upon torment, that wailing outcry; while you are suffering from this, and from your fear of death, shame added to that suffering with the shameful craft of the old wives who know about that painful ordeal, whose help is necessary to you however indecent it may be; and there you must put up with whatever happens to you.)¹⁷

I quote this passage at length because it so amusingly (and in some cases accurately!) describes quite specifically the many physical and emotional torments the pregnant and laboring woman undergoes. It also articulates the very real worry over physical pain in childbirth, and the fear of death that accompanies the anticipation and event of labor. Like some of the later male-authored midwifery manuals, it also instills in the young woman the fear of midwives; they are necessary, but their "creft" is "scheome" and "uncumelich," shameful and unbecoming. While *Hali Meidenhad* is designed to guide women to spiritual grace, it does so more through making them fear earthly experience of marriage, pregnancy, childbirth, and motherhood, than it does through prolific spiritual comforts.

While *Hali Meidenhad* uses the promise of freedom from earthly distress through virginity, the *Ancrene Wisse* offers anchoresses the guidelines for their daily practice based on the precepts of two types of rule: inner rule, charity, and outer rule, which governs the body in order to serve the other rule. Most of the text is dedicated to the inner rule of the heart, offering devotions for daily practice, means for protecting the heart from sin and temptations, and methods of confession. The very last part of the text suggests to the anchoress practical methods of maintaining the second rule, including what, how, and when to eat, dress and otherwise conduct themselves externally. For the purposes of this chapter, I look briefly at moments that explicitly address the dangers to the rule of the heart of lost virginity and idle chat. These dangers resonate with the culture's conflict between the virginal, seen here as anchoritic and isolated, and maternal, seen here as the visible, social, and open.

The two available roles for women are allegorized in Part Eight of the *Wisse* as two sisters, Mary and Martha. Mary is the sister who has chosen the life of enclosure, marked by silence and virginity; Martha is the sister who has chosen the life of a housewife, marked by social obligations such as gossip and childbirth. The author writes about these roles in relationship to how an anchoress must keep herself:

> Marie ant Marthe ba weren sustern, ah hare lif sundrede. ʒe ancren beod inumen ȝow to Marie dale, þe ure Laurerd seolf herede, "Maria optimam partem elegit." "Marthe, Marthe," quod he, "þu art in muche baret. Marie haueþ icore bet, ant ne schal hire na þing reauin hire dale." Husewifeshcipe is Marthe dale. Marie dale is stilnesse ant reste of alle worldes noise, þet na þing ne lette heren Godes steuene. Ant lokid hwet Godde seid, þet na þing ne schal ȝow reauin þis dale. Marthe haued hire meorster; leoted hire iwerden.[18]

> (Mary and Martha both were sisters, but their way of life diverged. You recluses have followed Mary's way, which Our Lord himself praised: 'Mary has chosen the best part.' 'Martha, Martha,' he said, 'you are in a great bustle, Mary has chosen better, and nothing will take her part away from her.' Being a housewife is Martha's part. Mary's part is silence and peace from all the noise of the world, so that nothing may prevent her

from hearing God's voice. And look what God says, that nothing will take this part away from you. Martha has her role; let her be.)[19]

The author of the *Wisse* suggests that there are two paths from which a woman can choose, the role of anchoress, as illustrated through Mary, and the role of a housewife, as illustrated through Martha. The role of Mary, the recluse, is the exalted "optimum" role, which allows for access to God's voice, and removal from "alle worldes noise." The role of Martha, on the other hand, involves taking care of livestock, dealing with people, and being in "baret," or turmoil.[20]

The dangers of the public path, of Martha, are made known through a discussion of how to see and be seen by others and the potential for being tempted from virginity, and through a discussion of proper dalliance practices and the potential for being drawn into gossip and idle chatter. The author warns that the act of seeing and being seen makes women vulnerable to sin: "as hit teleð i Genesy, eode ut to bihalden uncuðe wummen. Ʒet ne seid hit nawt þet ha biheold wepmen. Ant hwet come wenset tu of þat bihaldunge? Ha leas hire meidenhad ant wes imaket hore." (As it is told in Genesis, [Dinah] walked out to behold the strange women. Yet it does not tell that she beheld men. And what comes do you think of that beholding? She lost her maidenhead and was marked a whore.)[21] In this example to the anchoresses, just going out to look at "uncuðe wummen" amounts to the loss of virginity, and even a descent into whoredom. In this passage, being involved even tangentially with a female community can lead to physical, and therefore spiritual, defilement.

This anxiety over what happens when women get together is further illustrated in the author's advice to the anchoress on the appropriate methods of verbal interaction with those outside her anchorhold, suggesting that the sins that come from the eye may equally come from the mouth. He instructs that when someone comes to visit at her window she should first inquire from her maiden who it is, and then "crossið ful eome muð" (cross full your mouth).[22] She is then instructed to listen, but not speak: "hercnið hise wordes and halded ʒow al stille. þan hwen he parted from os, þen he ne cunne ower god, ne owe uuel no der" (hear his wordes and hold yourself entirely silent, so that when he parts from you, then he cannot your good, nor your evil [know].)[23] The idea is that the man should take nothing away from the encounter with the anchoress; somehow her silence ensures her integrity (*integritas*). He further advises "Ʒe mine leoue sustren folhið ure leasfdi, ant nawt te cakele eue" (You, my dear sisters, follow our Lady, and not the cackling Eve); it is Eve's chattering with the snake, so the author explains, that brought women to denigration.[24]

Likewise, this advice is also extended to the women who attend the anchoress, suggesting an anxiety about the nature of how women behave when they are together. The maidservants, for example, are not to bring any "idele talen ne neowe tidinges…ouer alle þinges, leasunges ant lidere wordes heatien" (idle stories or tidings of news…over all things, they should hate lies and evil words).²⁵ Bringing "idele" or worldly stories is potentially dangerous, as when Dinah steps outside to view the "uncuđe" women. Hearing evil words, like seeing men or strange women, can also lead to a corruption of the "heart." The anxiety that surfaces in the story of Dinah witnessing the strange women, resulting in her becoming a whore, is echoed also in the author's directions to the anchoress' maidservants, albeit without explicitly resulting in whoredom. Interestingly, he directs that the women who attend the anchoress "eider ligge ane" (each alone should sleep), suggesting an anxiety that women together have the potential of creating female communities that might be threatening to the careful construction of the anchorhold and its tenants.²⁶

THE EVERYDAY PRACTICE OF AN ANCHORITE

While Julian does not specifically describe her daily anchoritic practice, she appears to follow the general rule of anchoresses as laid out in *Ancrene Wisse*. She in many respects seems perfectly enclosed; she does not chat idly with other women or interact with female communities in any way, and she is, of course, chaste, and so is not threatening in a reproductive way. Nevertheless, the overall trajectory of Julian's sixteen revelations resembles a metaphorical birth, beginning with the onset of her illness in her darkened, womb-like room, through her vision of the bloody Christ, culminating with Revelation 15, in which she presents a degenerate swollen body and a pure birth. (The sixteenth revelation is simply the "conclusion and confirmation" to the fifteen preceding ones.) This metaphorical parturition is mostly—but not entirely—devoid of physiological attributes, and instead is cast partially in masculinized terms; in Julian's text, birth happens only in connection with Christ, and it is through Christ that birth is made positive. It is the implications of this imagery that I want to examine. Through this metaphorical process, Julian constructs a discourse on the maternity of God and Christ. She accomplishes this through her simultaneous alienation from, and attraction to, bodily birth, as evidenced by her occasional use of metaphors of birth within the overall structure, and her seeming disinterest in her own material existence.²⁷ Through the proliferation of instances in which she imagines God as maternal, as "our very mother," Julian suggests that she has a particular desire to construct a "perfect mother."²⁸ In recreating birth in its most culturally acceptable form—paternal Creation—Julian represents the maternal nature of God and Christ, where God and Christ are nurturers to whom she turns for guidance and comfort.²⁹ Nevertheless, they are represented as male Creators with maternal or feminine attributes, rather than as female procreators.³⁰ Thus, Julian expresses an unconscious desire to construct the procreative female body in patristic terms by situating and casting images of birth into an accepted location—that is by projecting them into functions of God or Christ.

In addition, the birth and menstruation metaphors Julian uses to describe her spiritual epiphanies and revelations give us an opportunity to examine some of the social practices of reproductive ritual and some of the medical notions of women. Her text does not carry a unified "message" about women's spiritual relationship with God as a form of subversion, nor does it represent a single system about the female anchorite's relationship to the procreative body. Rather, there are occasional images drawn from the female practice of birth—which mostly fall short of actual birth—which she uses, however inconsistently, to describe her connection with the feminine nature of God and the masculinized metaphors of birth.

In her essay "In the Meydens Womb: Julian of Norwich and the Poetics of Enclosure," Maud Burnett McInerney argues that Julian "reveals a fascination with the most inalienably female aspect of motherhood: the act of giving birth."[31] McInerney focuses on moments in which Julian represents Christ's Passion as labor and where these labors result in the birth of mankind. Nevertheless, while Julian shows a fascination with giving birth, this text is not entirely about the "inalienably female" process of birth, but rather is also about a desire to draw the (female) procreative experience either into or out of Godly creation. Julian's enclosure is an indication of her conscious decision not to participate in childbirth. It also reflects a certain alienation from the physical birth process of birth in its culturally practiced form. Julian's avoidance of physical birth and her near obsession with seeing God as maternal lead to some remarkable representations, many of which evolve out of the notion of divine birth.

"DEAD FROM THE MIEDES DOWNWARD"

Julian theologizes maternity in part through representing her spiritual revelations in terms of a metaphoric birth in which she sets up God as the perfect mother. In addition, Julian's text in its physiologic images and metaphors shadows female birth rituals, female communities, and the female bodily experience. These images occur around the occasion of Julian's own bodily illnesses that precede and result in the onset of her revelations. In the beginning of her text, Julian expresses a desire to have three things: the "mind of the passion," "bodily sickness," and "God's gift of three wounds," all of which circulate around the physical experience of pain, and some of which are represented at times, as McInerney has suggested, in terms of labor.[32] The pain and bodily sickness she desires she often expresses in images of female reproductive physiology, while she simultaneously tries to deny or escape the bodily through images or experiences of the spiritual or the ghostly. In addition, the "space" and manner in which Julian receives her bodily sickness at times resemble the space and practice of female rituals of birth. In fact, Julian's description of her illness bears traces of the birth ritual: the laboring woman is separated in a room that is enclosed and darkened except for candles, after many hours and sometimes days of labor, the woman gives birth, after which she follows a procedure of reintegration (as described in Chapter One). In Julian's case, her labor, or illness, produces revelations, a spiritual birth, rather than a literal one.

For example, Julian describes her surroundings as follows: "It waxid darke aboute me in the chamber as if it had ben nyght, saue in the image of the crosse, wher in held a comon light."[33] The room, like a birthing space, is dark, save for a light which comes inexplicably from the crucifix that is held by her curate, who acts as a kind of midwife to her revelations. Julian's description of her physical travails resembles those of labor:

> Thus I indured till day, and by then was my body dead from the miedes downward, as to my feeling. Then was I holpen to be set vpright, vndersett with helpe...My most payne was shortnes of breth... And in this sodenly all my paine was taken from me, and I was as hole, and namely in þe over parte of my bodie.[34]

Her physical pain (labor) gives way to a numbness and shortness of breath (delivery). There is even mention of her being helped to sit upright, which is suggestive of the ritual of upsitting after delivery which is followed later by complete relief (post-partum) in the "over parte" (Crampton's manuscript edition reads "other parte"). These images give a small idea of how it appears women dealt socially with their procreative bodies. In her echoing of childbirth, we get a deeper sense of the intensity of Julian's physical travails as she experiences her visions.

Julian experiences this "bodily sickness" for three days and nights before her first revelation. During this time she believes "by the feelyng of my paynes" that she will die, echoing the sentiment expressed in *Hali Meidenhad* in which women are warned that they will experience "in the birthing, the strongest of all pains, and sometimes death." In fearing death, Julian takes the last rites on the fourth night, but she endures until daylight, at which point her "bodie [is] dead from the miedes downward, as to my feeling."[35] Julian's description of her physical pain is similar in its physiological dimensions to that of labor in childbirth. The pain seems to be as much pain as she can stand (women often report feeling as if they would die), and she is not quite "present" in her body, on the contrary, a kind of physical "absence" seems to be required in order for her revelations to talk place.[36] Further, the focus on her body in pain becomes a focus on her numbed body, and the numbness is focused on the specific area that is "from the miedes downward." While this numbness could have many physiological sources, this representation of her "miedes" or "middle" as "dead" draws attention to Julian's procreative potential while at the same time emphasizing her decision not to procreate. Her "middle" exists, and yet it is without effect; it has procreative possibilities, yet remains chaste. Insofar as it represents these things, Julian projects the culture's conflicting desire for her to be fruitful and at the same time chaste.

The Bloody Garland

After all of her pain is taken from her, "and I was as hele," Julian "suddenly" has a thought in which she desires the "felyng of His blissed passion."[37] With this desire comes her first revelation, which is of the "crownyng" of Christ at his Crucifixion. During this revelation, Julian draws on very vivid images of excessive bleeding to recount her experience of Christ's labors on the Cross. Elizabeth Robertson, in her essay "Medieval Medical Views," argues that Julian draws specifically on the medieval medical theory of humors to express the physicality of Christ; she also argues that Julian's revelations "spring from experiences of the body" and are therefore "distinctively feminine."[38] While Robertson has argued that Julian's image of a sensual and physical Christ is about her identification with Christ and herself "as God incarnate," I would like to suggest that Julian not only uses physical, maternal attributes to identify her spirituality with Christ (and thereby God), she also uses Christ and God as a means to masculinize her metaphorical birth. It is in this way she comes to her first revelation "hele" or whole, virginal, to contemplate Christ's wounds and labor. The separation of her feminine maternal spirit allows her to rise above the earthly to the heavenly.

She reveals this connection most notably in her first revelation where, in a depleted physical state, she contemplates Christ's body on the crucifix. This first revelation is important because it is so graphic and bound so closely to the experience of the body. Coming as it does "without anie meane," without any intermediary, enhances the immediacy of the vision and suggests a private relationship between Julian and Christ.[39] Like the above passage that suggests childbirth even while eliding it, her revelations also reveal an association in her mind between "lively bleeding" and the rebirth that Christ's blood makes possible. This life blood could be associated with the other birth images in that it follows the birth, when all her pain was taken from her. Julian's projects a bloody excess onto Christ as she imagines Christ bleeding relentlessly on the Cross:

> And in this sodenly I saw the reed bloud rynnyng downe from vnder the garlande, hote and freyshely, plentuously and liuely, right as it was in the tyme that the garland of thornes was pressed on his blessed head.[40]

After her sudden revival from her "deadly" living body, Julian finds herself in the presence of a lively dying body. She describes the blood that is running down from under Christ's garland as "hot" and "freshly," which gives a sense of immediate presence of life. Julian also reports this vision "as it was in the time that the garland of thorns was pressed on his blessed head," further suggesting its physical immediacy and her presence in the event. That the blood is "plenteous" as well as "lively" suggests that this blood is both excessive and quick moving. Robertson specifically sees the excess of blood from Christ's head as being like menstrual blood when it is purged from the body which, according to humoral theory, must occur in order to keep a balance between the bodily humors. She suggests this representation is connected to Julian's "own natural purgation of excess," as well as a representation of the femininity of Christ.[41] I would further argue that this focus on the image of Christ's purgation suggests not just the femininity of Christ, but the cleansing of Julian's own femininity—and at a time when she seems removed from her body through her numbing illness.[42] This excessive blood, rather than being associated with the curse of menstruation, is here connected with the positive, salvific attributes of salvation. The physicality of the excess blood, which, on the one hand, signals Julian as "distinctively feminine" in her focus on female physiology, also indicates Julian's desire to associate herself physiologically to Christ. Ironically, Julian's sickness is followed by images of menstruation (purgation), which also suggest a lack of pregnancy and absence of childbirth.

The image of Christ's garland emitting large quantities of blood recurs in the first revelation, and the second episode is even more graphic than the first:

> I saw the bodely syght lastyng of the (plentuous) bledyng of the hede. The grett droppes of blode felle downe fro vnder the garlonde lyke pelottes, semyng as it had comynn ouȝte of the veynes. And in the comyng ouȝte they were browne rede, for the blode was full thycke; and in the spredyng abrode they were bryght rede.[43]

Robertson notes that this passage is "even more evocative of menstrual blood" in its specific description than the previous passage.[44] The blood is "full thick" and "brown red," and then "bright red" as it "spreads abroad...seeming as it had come out of the veins." In attributing such female physiological characteristics to the dying Christ—who enables our rebirth like a midwife enables birth—Julian further identifies Christ with the feminine, and, conversely, masculinizes menstruation. These maternal or feminine attributes of menstruation and purgation not only reaffirm the physicality of Christ, but they also serve to remind us of Julian's struggle with her own "femaleness." While the plentiful bleeding and the ever-advancing blood have an overwhelming quality to it, it is one that is linked to Julian's spiritual elation at her vision of Christ.

THE FAMILY OF THE TRINITY

In a later revelation, Julian grapples with "our" relationship to the Holy Trinity; a relationship that is familial in nature, and full of slippery descriptions of our holy origins. The spiritual family of the feminized Christ and idealized Maternity of God and the Holy Trinity as constructed by Julian give her deep satisfaction and fulfillment throughout her revelations. Julian employs the maternity of God and of the Holy Trinity through the image of the Trinity as closed or enclosed. Her use of these images suggests both

Theologized Maternity in Julian of Norwich's Book of Showings

a replacement of masculine (physiologic) images of Creation with that of feminine images of the enclosed womb, as well as a masculinized family structure that is creative rather than procreative:

> For the almyghty truth of the trynyte is oure fader, for he made vs and kepyth vs in him. And the depe wysdome of þe trynyte is our moder, in whom we be closyd. And the hye goodness of the trynyte is our lord, and in hym we be closyd and he in vs. We be closyd in the fader, and we be closyd in the son, and we are closyd in the holy gost. And the fader is beclosyd in vs, the son is beclosyd in vs, and the holy gost is beclosyd in vs.[45]

Here Julian represents her, and "our," relationship to God and the Holy Trinity as that of a child to its parents. When she writes that the "truth of the Trinity is our father, for he made us and kepyth us in him. And the deep wisdom of the Trinity is our mother, in whom we be closed," she couples the maternal role with the patristic creative one. In this passage, as opposed to the above one, Julian puts a finer point on our "enclosure" in God, Christ, and the Holy Ghost, for we "be closyd" in all three, and all three are "beclosed in us." In addition to constructing an image of a spiritual gestation and Creation from God and a rebirth through Christ, Julian also constructs an image of physical, womb-like gestation within which she seeks comfort.

Julian also sets up the Trinity as the framework within which her relationship to Christ and God occurs, and through which she is made. She works out the familial relationship between the Trinity and herself, but God alone is not the agent, for Julian suggests the traditional father-mother union is necessary for creation when she connects the father with "the deep wisdom of the trinity is our mother, in whom we are closed." Here we are also "enclosed" in the mother, an image that suggests the womb. Finally, she locates us in a loop-the-loop of enclosures: "the high goodness of the trinity is our lord, and in him we are closed and he in us. And the father is beclosed in us, the son is beclosed in us, and the holy ghost is beclosed in us." This particular configuration suggests that a collapse occurs between the bearer and the born, the encloser (the womb) and the enclosed. Given the ways Julian transfers birth imagery to a metaphorical sphere in the previous (and following) section, it makes sense that a passage like this would also be riddled with a strange collapsing of maternity with paternity, and the container with the contained. And of course the repetition of "closyd" and "beclosyd" describes more than "a relationship between container and contained; it also evokes the tradition of anchoritism," a tradition in which Julian was wholly engaged in, and at the same time reformulated through her use of maternal images.[46]

Of Clean Deliverance

The first fifteen of Julian's revelations take place over the course of one day, culminating in a vision that represents the birth of our soul through a metaphoric earthly birth—the sixteenth revelation occurs the following day. Julian begins Revelation 15 by setting up the image of Christians as being God's children being born and dying into God: "Thus I vnderstode that all his blessyd chyldren whych be come out of hym by kynd shulde be brougt agayne in to hym by grace."[47] While the text suggests that the children "come out" of God, this image is not so much supposed to be about God giving birth—although it certainly is suggestive of that—as it is about God's creative, or originary power. "Be come" suggests that his children "become" or originate out of God, as well as suggesting that they "do come" out of him (*OED* s.v. def. 26: to come, in reference to origin). Julian then describes her desire to be "delivered" from this world (that is, to die): "...I had grete longyng and desyr of goddys gyfte to be delyuerde of this worlde and of this lyfe."[48] Julian's desire to die is really a desire to be born into eternal life, a rebirth in which Christ acts as a kind of midwife to "deliver" Julian to eternity. God tells Julian that she will be taken from the world suddenly and will no longer suffer bodily discomfort or illness—something that Julian both desires to have and be rescued from. Julian's deliverance or "re-birth" here occurs through the agency of God and Christ, and also removes Julian from the location of the body. While Julian constructs God and Jesus as maternal in the text as a whole, she does not in fact see them as female insofar as they do not labor or suffer pain in childbirth.

After Julian describes her desire to be delivered to God, she presents what is one of her most amazing metaphorical visions of birth. Julian consciously interprets this vision as a metaphor for the struggle between our deadly flesh (as symbolized by the swollen body) and our pure soul (symbolized by the child). On the one hand, the use of this trope as such depicts Julian's overall desire to convey the suffering and plight of the human body in relation to the role of the soul in general. On the other hand, her use of an image that is suggestive of childbirth also indicates a particular relationship between the swollen and maternal body. Further, although it is one of the few explicit images of bodily birth in her text, it suggests the impurity and practice of physical birth and attempts to purge that impurity explicitly.[49] This passage, more than any other, reveals Julian's own discomfort with the body and birth. Colledge and Walsh's edition from MS NB Fonds anglais 40 is collated with MSS MB Sloan 2499 and 3705, so that the vision reads thus:

> And in thys tyme I sawe a body lyeng on þe erth, whych body shewde heuy and feerfulle and with oute shape and forme, as it were a swylge stynkyng myrre; and sodeynly oute of this body sprong a fulle feyer creature, a lyttlle chylld, full shapyn and formyd, swyft and lyfly and whytter then the lylye, whych sharpely glydyd vppe in to hevyn.[50]

Julian's vision of a body "lying on the earth," in a "heavy and fearful" state, suggests a female body that is full of fear as well as causing fear. The other existing seventeenth-century manuscript that contains Julian's full text, found in editions edited by Marion Glascoe and Georgia Ronan Crampton, describes the body using the words "hevy and oggley," attributing to the pregnant female body ugliness.

While the birthing body is described as "it" and without any female referents, its gender is nonetheless implied through not only its function, but through the "feminine" nature of its representation. That which is "earthly" is necessarily base, and Julian conflates the body with the foul earth it lies upon. She describes the body with foul and sinful images of sin, of a "stynkyng myrre." Even while she recognizes it as a "heavy" (and presumably pregnant) body, she denies it contour, describing it as "without shape and form." Something without shape or form must take the form of its container, which in this case is the earth. She also reveals in this passage some of the cultural notions of women's reproductive nature. In describing the pregnant woman as having neither shape nor form, as simply existing as a kind of malleable vessel, Julian expresses and adheres to the common notions of medical theories of conception and pregnancy, in which the female provides the matter, the male the form.[51] This act of attempting to occlude the pregnant female body while simultaneously imagining it further reveals Julian's complex relationship to it.

Significantly, at the moment when Julian is describing the "body" as it is about to give birth, the modernized language of the seventeenth-century text becomes more archaic, using, instead of modernized versions of Julian's language, language resembling that of Julian's own era. Colledge and Walsh have suggested in the notes to their edition of Julian's text that "this is the closest that Julian comes to the language of her times in describing the miseries of the flesh."[52] This scribal archaism suggests that the scribes may have had their own difficulty with the language at the point when Julian herself exhibits difficulty with the birthing female body. The scribes of the modernized seventeenth-century *Book of Showings*, in offering traces of perhaps Julian's original but archaic language, reveal their own alienation from Julian's era as well as her metaphorical image of the procreating body. Specifically, at the moment of the "birth" the text reads: "whych body shewde with oute shape and forme, as it were a swylge stynkyng myrre; and sodeynly oute of this body sprong a fulle feyer creature." The phrase "swylge stynkyng myrre" is problematic, especially "swylge." The words "swylge" or "myrre" are otherwise unattested. The glosses and marginalia found in the manuscript used by Colledge and Walsh note "swylge" to mean "foul." The etymology, which is difficult to determine because the origin of the word "swylge" isn't specifically identifiable, suggests that "swylge" may come from "swallow," "swollen," and then "swill" (*OED*, "swallow" def. 1a, 2; n."swollen" def.1).[53]

The alternate manuscript version sheds some light on this difficult phrase, which seems to have perplexed modern-day transcribers as well as seventeenth-century scribes. As mentioned above, the manuscript editions transcribed and edited by Glascoe and Crampton present a slightly different version: "which body shewid hevy and oggley withoute shappe and forme, as it were a bolned quave of styngand myre."[54] Marginal notes in this manuscript version gloss "bolned" as "puffed up" and "quave" as "quaggmire."[55] Hence, this stinking, pregnant mass is both swollen ("bolned," "swylge") and empty like a pit ("myre," "quave"), where the pit of the "quave" could be an image of a womb. Julian, in using images of the swollen in juxtaposition with the stinking "myrre" or pit, suggests an understanding of pregnancy and birth as earthly and foul; *Hali Meidenhad* also equates pregnancy with foulness, as we have seen. The coupling also suggests a conflation of the swollen with the empty.

While the feminine, earthly body that Julian associates with birth is foul, and the pregnant body fearful, the infant that comes from that body is the pure soul:

> and sodeynly oute of this body sprong a fulle feyer creature, a lyttlle chylld, full shapyn and formyd, swyft and lyfly and whytter then the lylye, whych sharpely glydyd vppe in to hevyn.[56]

Very suddenly, without any physical pain or labor, a "full fair creature" springs from the body. This little child not only has agency that the formless body that births it lacks—it is not born but springs out of the body—but it is "fully shaped and formed." It is not a heavy, ugly, stinking pit of a creature lying on the earth, but rather a swift, lively, pure little child that "sharply glides up to heaven." In her interpretation of this vision, Julian further tries to separate the physical "wretchedness" of the body from the pureness of the soul:

> The swylge of the body betokenyth grette wretchydness of oure dedely flessch; and the lyttlnes of the chylde betokenyth the clennes and the puernesse of oure soule. And I thought: with thys body blyueth no feyernesse of thys chylde, ne of this chylde dwellyth no foulnes of the body.[57]

While the swollen body "represents the great wretchedness of our deadly flesh," the "littleness of the child represents the purity of our soul." The "deadly flesh," like the swollen body, is associated with the wretched flesh, and so the female body contrasts to the perfection and purity found in the soul.[58] Julian could not draw a starker contrast between the lowliness of the birthing body and the purity of the child who is "whiter than the lily." And while she demonstrates through this contrast a desire to separate physical being and birth from spiritual purity, she also constructs them as interdependent and inextricably linked: the infant's existence is always predicated on its mother, as the soul, it seems, on the body.[59]

This birth image has a strange relationship to the images that Julian sets up in earlier parts of these revelations in which God is figured as our "deer-worthy mother," and in which we "be come out of hym" in a (highly) symbolic birth. That is, in contrast to the Creative rather than procreative image of birth—in which any trace of body is (by necessity) elided and in which we both come out of and go back into God the mother—this birth requires that the "child" go away from the swollen physical mother not to return. Julian needs to remove the body from the child and the child from the body: "With this body remains no fairness of this child, nor of this child dwells no foulness of the body." Paradoxically, by focusing on the sharp distinction between the earth-bound flesh of the body and the heaven-bound intactness of the soul, Julian ends up turning to the fleshly aspects of birth, especially as they get articulated in *Hali Meidenhad* which describes childbirth and marriage as "so low alighted, into fleshly filth, into the life of a beast."[60] In all her insistence on God's bodiless maternity, Julian cannot help but explore bodily maternity, even while she theologizes it. She can strip feminine fleshliness from the maternal in God's creation of us, but she cannot, perhaps will not, strip the fleshliness from the maternal in the procreation of the body.

Instead of focusing on Mary's virgin birth of Christ, or Christ's delivery of us from our sins, Julian engages in a matrix of metaphors, with Mary as our mother, Christ our very mother, and a labor that is never realized. The non-bodily birth incorporates imagery of perpetual labor and delivery, an anxiety evoked by texts like *Hali Meidenhad* and which must have been present in any potentially procreative woman.[61] This perpetual delivery can best be seen in Revelation 14. Julian interrogates the relationship to birth and maternity of the Creation further, again describing our own spiritual "origins." At this point in the text Julian presents a genealogy of Creation and of our faith. She describes how God "knytt" Christ to "oure body in the meydens wombe":

> Thus oure lady is oure moder, in whome we be all beclosyd and of hyr borne in Crist, for she that is moder of oure savyoure is mother of all þat ben savyd in oure sauyour; and our sauyoure is oure very moder, in whome we be endlesly borne and nevyr shall come out of hym.[62]

This passage reflects a complex relationship of pregnancies and maternities—the motherhood of Mary and Christ as well as ourselves, and then birth, and the lack of birth. Mary ("oure lady") is our mother, in whom we are "all beclosed," an image that suggests that we are enclosed within her womb. Yet Julian describes us as "of her borne in Christ"; that is, in as much as we have been saved by Christ, we are born of her, for Christ is born of Mary. Maternity here does not rest with "our mother," though she is Christ's mother, but rather with "our very mother" who is Christ himself. Further, Julian, in describing our birth from Christ as "in whom we are endlessly borne and never shall come out of him," occludes bodily birth, in which the birth and delivery is continuous. This could also be an image of labor in which we are never delivered, "we...never shall come out of him," and in which we remain enclosed in Christ. From this, Julian projects her own desires for and practice of enclosure, for a sanctified place represented by the "womb" of Christ, in which she is endlessly delivered, but never born.[63] It is a desire that can only be realized in a theologized, bodily maternity.

Julian's spiritual desires and ideologies are clearly connected to and mediated by her sense of the maternal female body. Through these images of the maternal body we can appreciate the elements in the culture's apprehension of the potentially procreative body. Also through these images we can see certain elements of the social practice of childbirth in its uneasy, but seemingly inextricable, relationship to female devotional practice. Julian's devotional practice and revelatory experiences mirror and at times seek to resist the culture's model of female devotional and social, procreative practice. On the one hand, her representations of the female reproductive body that I have described in this chapter are in alignment with the culture's anxieties about female procreation. On the other hand, her use of these maternal images to represent Christ and God suggests the power of a female maternal subjectivity that resists and at least occasionally subverts the masculine structure of Creativity. Revisiting her dalliance with Julian in *The Book of Margery Kempe* for a moment, we are reminded of Margery's very worldly expression of her spiritual devotions, methods which sometimes met with the kind of resistance absent from Julian's. Likewise, Margery's earthly knowledge of childbirth and her desire for abstinence surface in very different ways in her spiritual visions and insights.

CHAPTER 3
A Very Maternal Mysticism
Images of Childbirth and Its Rituals in *The Book of Margery Kempe*[1]

In the first chapter of *The Book of Margery Kempe* we learn that Margery was twenty years old when she married the burgess of Lynn, after which she immediately had a child.[2] Her pregnancy was a difficult one, and she suffered attacks of sickness until the baby was born. Because her labor was so difficult and because she was sick throughout her pregnancy, she believed that after her baby was born she was going to die. For six months following the birth of her first child, we are told, she was tormented with spirits until the time when Christ came to her in a vision and restored her to her wits.[3] After the first chapter, there is not much the *Book* tells us about Margery's earthly pregnancies or birth experiences. Further, nothing is revealed about this firstborn child nor the other thirteen children to whom she gives birth; we only have an account of one son's salvation in his adulthood in the second book. Scholars such as Wendy Harding have also noticed the "paucity of references to Margery's life as a mother."[4] This apparent repression could clearly come out of her desire throughout the text to remain celibate, to resist the culturally prescribed duties of mothering for those not of a traditional, enclosed mystic, but one who actively seeks the company of others with whom to share her spiritual revelations. Even though Margery throughout her text struggles to remain celibate and lives, for the most part, separate from her husband and family, she nonetheless conducts a life in which childbirth and marriage play a significant part, as opposed to Julian who rejects these things altogether (as seen in the previous chapter). Like Julian, Margery exhibits in her work a movement to transform social experience into a more idyllic visionary one. Her visionary experiences are revised (idyllic) versions of inadequate social situations, some of which have to do with childbirth and reproduction. Yet while Julian's metaphoric transformations of childbirth are often convoluted and obscure, Margery's are more straightforward, transparent. Despite the fact that the *Book* contains very little about Margery's fourteen children, her contemplations repeatedly reenact the maternal experiences of Mary, St. Anne, and Elizabeth, rehearsing birth and mothering through images and metaphors.

It is not surprising to find that Kempe's *Book* has been the location of many critical inquiries. Scholars have been interested in the kinds of contributions it has made to our knowledge of the female mystical experience, to the bodily experience of women in religious life, and to notions of the body and the construction of the feminine in general. Some scholars are interested in whether or not the *Book* can be read as a subversive one through which Margery's abject mystical experience represents a kind of empowerment, or a construction of female subjectivity. Other scholars, such as Sarah Beckwith, Carolyn Walker Bynum, and Karma Lochrie (to name a few), have variously concluded, either explicitly or implicitly, that the *Book* cannot finally break free from masculine definitions and constructions of the feminine.[5] In the course of their work on Margery's interest in "ghostly births," Bynum and Gail McMurray Gibson have linked Margery's interest in "iconographic motifs" of the Visitation, of Mary, and of Christ's birth and life to her biological nature because these narratives "responded to women's interests." Bynum also suggests that "it is possible that there is a biological element in women's predisposition to certain kinds of bodily experiences."[6] Along these lines, Gibson suggests Margery's "fascination with the holy event of Nativity involves her own intimate knowledge of the rites of conception and childbirth."[7]

What has been left largely unexamined is the cultural conflict that gets enacted through the facts of physical and metaphorical mothering. Drawing together social and medical history with literary analysis, this chapter looks at how the *Book* expresses and negotiates the conflict between the female procreative body and the ideal virginal body through Margery's representations of her spiritual practices. While texts like *Trotula* and *The Byrth of Mankynde* directly address reproductive practices, Margery's representational text tends to avoid or repress them. Through the recurrence of visions that are accompanied by social elements of the birth ritual, Margery, as well as her transcriber, demonstrates ways in which maternity was desirable and at the same time anxiety provoking for medieval Christian women. Margery also shows through these metaphors a desire to simultaneously excuse herself from and control and liberate women's procreative bodies generally. She draws to the center her procreative body, and she rewrites its history; she succeeds in this "rewriting" through her "visionary participation in Incarnation history."[8] While Margery cannot change the dominant symbols of virginity and the fruitful body that she relies on to mediate her experiences of piety, she can and does use the dominant discourses of Christ's life and Passion, and the Virgin Mary's maternity, to tell more than the story of God and Christ. Her maternal visions widen her communities beyond the traditional earthly birth communities (although presumably she has those, too). Further, in these visions and in the course of her travels and experiences, female devotional, textual, and birth communities get imagined and constructed.

Throughout the *Book*, Margery expresses a desire for a configuration that does not exist in the culture. On the one hand, she aspires to be holy and sanctified, as evidenced by her meditations and devotions to God that drive the *Book*'s production. On the other hand, she participates as a family member, a wife and mother, as evidenced by her marriage, her fourteen children, and her return to her husband in his time of illness late in her life. The various social and visionary experiences in Margery's text that relate to familial organizations make clear that the maternal and the virginal cannot comfortably coexist except in the visionary community. I examine here some of the modulations between social and visionary events in Margery's life that reenact or seek to recreate maternal experiences. Because of the complex manner in which Margery's *Book* was produced, through multiple male scribes and over a period of years, it is impossible to know exactly in what order the episodes of Margery's life occur or how they might have been reconstructed by either her amanuensis or herself. Thus, these modulations cannot be seen as having a particular chronological significance. Rather, certain episodes touch variously on the themes of pain in childbirth, female communities, and male intercessors.

PAIN IN CHILDBIRTH

Julian of Norwich, in the beginning of her *Book of Showings* experiences in her enclosure, just prior to the onset of her revelations, a grave illness from which she believes she will die (she even receives the last rites). Likewise, just before her profane visions, Margery experiences an illness that relates to the birth of her first child in which she also feels the need to call for her confessor. Unlike Julian, however, Margery's illness draws on her lived experience of pain in childbirth. Her childbirth, which is followed first by an unsatisfactory visit from her confessor, then profane and finally sacred visions, is the initiating event of what results in visionary reconfigurations of pain in childbirth.

To begin, the maternal images present in these events draw our attention both to the real and symbolic constructions of gender and sexual identity; motherhood in the narrowest sense can be seen as a biological distinction and division in which women are "individually and collectively engaged in these physical facts of motherhood."[9] Julia Kristeva has suggested that women have access to the Imaginary and the pre-linguistic through this specific biological experience of giving birth, an access that I would argue hinges in part on the particular experience of pain in childbirth.[10] Elaine Scarry has shown us that pain in general "does not simply resist language but actively destroys it, bringing about an immediate reversion to a state anterior to language, to the sounds and cries a human being makes before language is learned."[11] While Scarry does not speak specifically to pain in childbirth, her formulations are applicable here. This is one way of situating the female experience of birth as occurring beyond the boundaries of language. Of course, pain in childbirth is somewhat unique in its physical and psychological elements in that it is predictably periodic in both senses of the word. Labor pains generally occur at regular intervals, with nearly a complete absence of pain between contractions, then gradually increase in intensity until the birth, ending at the time the uterus returns to near-normal size. (The knowledge that the pain is periodic and represents the eminent arrival of the child is thought to make the pain more tolerable.)

The account given of Margery's first birth suggests that the physical experience of childbirth was not always a pleasant one, and indeed texts like *Hali Meidenhad*, the "Sekenesse of Wymmen," and *Trotula* support this (the physical *experience* of pregnancy and childbirth—in its cultural and "scientific" constructions—seems to remain essentially constant). Margery's anxiety about dying after childbirth is also confirmed in these obstetrical manuals, as well as in later texts such as *The Monument of Matrones* where women specifically voice the fear that they or their infant will die in childbirth. The experience expressed in Margery Kempe's text about the event of childbirth was common among women of medieval and early modern Europe and was grounded in infant and maternal mortality rates. Some argue that maternal mortality rates in childbirth may have been as high as 15 to 20 percent,[12] others argue that it may have been much lower, from 1 to 2 percent (although higher in the seventeenth century, and in London).[13] Margery's opening birth experience also illustrates well the emotional and spiritual travails that come with pregnancy and childbirth, including, as Harding has suggested, a woman's deep understanding and "recognition of her own sinfulness."[14]

In addition to a long and difficult labor, many women experienced illnesses during their pregnancies. The sickness that begins as a physical illness of pregnancy ends up with Margery in a spiritual crisis, drawing the fears of the spirit and the bodily together. Margery conflates pregnancy, labor, and birth into one representation, highlighting these fears and ailments in this one experience:

> And, aftyr sche had conceyued, sche was labowrd wyth grett accessys tyl þe chyld was born, & þan, what for labowr sche had in chyldyng & for sekeness goyng beforn, sche dyspered of hyr lyfe, wenyn sche mygth not leuyn.[15]

After Margery conceives, she "labored with great excess until the child was born," suggesting that she labored throughout her entire pregnancy. She fears that the "labowr" and "sekeness" she endured while she was pregnant, which equates to the labor of childbirth itself, will continue post partum, and because of this she fears that she will die.[16]

A Very Maternal Mysticism: Images of Childbirth and Its Rituals

In dealing with her fear of dying in childbirth, Margery represents the conflicting role of male intercessors in relation to women's secrets, here seen through confessions and childbirth. Having "dyspered of hyr lyfe," fearing she will die, Margery sends for her "confessor" because she has "a thyng in conscyens whech she had neuyr schewyd be-forn at tyme in alle hyr lyfe."[17] Margery greatly desires to absolve this "thyng" that she has in her conscience that has never been revealed to anyone before (and which is not revealed in the course of her text), and the confessor serves metaphorically here as a midwife to Margery's confession. The fact that we are told not of the actual birth, but rather hear about the necessity for a confessor, suggests that the confession of a sin is of greater value to the narrative than the story of the midwife, gossips, and mother who delivered the child.

Just as Margery's birth proves difficult, so her experience with her confessor proves inadequate for her needs. Margery is ultimately not able to reveal on her (believed) deathbed that which she was unwilling to reveal previously in her life; she would rather "don penawns be hir-self alonne."[18] Her desire to do her penance alone suggests her need to cut herself off from male judgment and dominance, in the same safe manner as she was in childbirth. When Margery is at the point of "seyn þat þing whech sche had so long conselyd, hir confessowr was a lytyl to hastye & gan scharply to vndyrnemyn hir."[19] This sharp admonition comes just at the point when Margery is about to reveal herself, suggesting that the confessor is ill equipped to perform this duty. He also functions as a metaphor for male intrusion into this sacred female community where information is exchanged, but not necessarily disseminated to the outside world. Instead of a flow of information (Margery's great secret), nothing is revealed. It seems as if Margery's fears about revealing this particular privity, which she simultaneously desires to do and is anxious about, are realized. Her inability to confess is as much a result of her confessor's apparent inadequacy as her unwillingness to reveal herself.

Sacred and Profane Visitations

While there is not always a one-to-one correspondence between a "real" event and a subsequent meditation, the profane and sacred visions that Margery has following the birth of her first child could be seen as a visionary response to the inadequacies and difficulties of these events. Her experience also suggests the connection between childbirth and the practice of Christian devotion, which extend to the potentially profane.[20] For example, Margery is described as being "owt of hir mende & was wondyrlye vexid & labowryd with spyritys" when she was unable to confess her sin.[21] While to labor with spirits means to struggle with them, the image of "labowryd with spyritys" suggests both a sinful birth (that is, giving birth to the devil) and an otherworldly labor. Later, her postpartum experience of revelation is punctuated by the visions that come to her fresh out of childbirth—of devils with gaping orifices and flaming, burning mouths: "deuyls opyn her mowthyus al inflaumyd wyth brennyng lowys of fyr."[22] In addition, this vision resonates eerily with the physical experience of birth; the open mouth suggests a dilated cervix, and the burning flames of fire echo the burning sensation that accompanies the baby passing through the vagina. This reading sees Kempe as unable to get away from her previous birth experience. This moment also suggests that her inability to reveal her verbal and corporeal privities to the proper recipient is a sin, leading to the "fire" of information out of the devil's mouth.

The profane visits are countered by the sacred when Christ comes to her in a vision. Margery is, again, in a private space; "she lay a-loone" in bed, thus extending the association of childbirth and the profane with the sacred. When Christ comes to her in the likeness of a beautiful man, "sche had long ben labowrd in þes & many oþer temptacyons."[23] Christ, like the confessor, appears after she has been in a long (and metaphorical) labor—this time with temptations. After Christ's visitation, however, she is not met with madness, but rather with reason.[24] Despite her return to rational behavior, the encounter, like many of the subsequent contemplations and visions she has of Christ, is riddled with images of desire and (symbolic as well as literal) penetration—Christ coming to Margery in the most beautiful presentation possible as she lies alone in her bed is suggestive of a seduction scene. Margery seems to be saying that male presence in women's space can be either holy (a confessor, priest, Christ) or profane (visions of the devil or evil spirits), but that each is an adulteration of some kind.

Margery refigures these visions in her subsequent meditations to include a female community that fills a need that she lacks in everyday life. Margery serves God through these meditational moments that also function to seal her off from the worldly and relieve her of certain "female" duties of procreation. Her meditations also show her desire for and her preoccupation with the maternal metaphors; in fact, she rather insists on them in several places in her text. Margery mimics the trajectory of birth through a reverie suggested to her by Christ, and through the events that occur in the chapters that follow this reverie (Chapters Six and Seven). The architecture and contents of these chapters suggests the ritual and process of childbirth. Margery, keeping in mind her excessive bodily sins, draws upon elements of sacred birth, including a metaphoric, Annunciation-like visitation from Christ that is developed using the images and language of childbirth ritual, of a sacred and sanctified gossiping, and of maternity. In rehearsing a "sacred" birth narrative, Margery shows a desire to recover the "virginal purity lost" in her own life.[25] The meditation is preceded by Christ inserting into Margery's mind certain thoughts that she will later reveal:

> I wyl þow leue þi byddyng of many bedys and thynk swych thowtys as I wyl putt in þi mend...& I byd þe gon to þe ankyr at Frer Prechowrys, and schew hym my preuyteys & my cownsel.[26]

A Very Maternal Mysticism: Images of Childbirth and Its Rituals

Here, Christ gives her "hey medytacyon" and contemplation through his private language, much the way the Virgin Mary received the Annunciation. Margery, like Mary, becomes a mediatrix of Christ's "privities" and counsel, therein initiating her imitation of the "culturally sanctioned model of motherhood" as defined by the Virgin Mary, an imitation which is part of the sacred revision of her birthing experience.[27] This construction of Christ putting thoughts into Margery's mind also reflects medieval notions of conception: Christ's words serve to create her experience—he supplies the form, she the matter.

FEMALE COMMUNITIES: BRINGING UP MARY

In her "hey medytacyon" Margery joins Julian in the anchoritic rejection of the body and in the banishment of a female community of the kind warned against in *Ancrene Wisse*. Margery also makes no mention of a female community in relation to the birth of her child in the first chapter; instead she develops a vision of a female community in her vision of St. Anne, Mary, and Elizabeth. Margery's perhaps unconscious desire to reconcile herself and her bodily experiences of pregnancy with the culture's discourses of virginity and holy motherhood lead her to replicate the birth of Mary. Mary, Anne, Elizabeth and Christ symbolize for Margery the perfect spiritual maternal paradigm—immaculate conception, virginal and painless birth, and the promise of resurrection. But in replicating this paradigm, she infuses the biblical nativities with her own social performance of childbirth. Thus, Margery manipulates these narratives to her own ends, which includes constructing a female community, and reworking, to some degree, biblical history. For example, in her visions of Anne's, Mary's, and Elizabeth's pregnancies and births, Margery acts as handmaiden, midwife, and nursemaid, thus both fitting herself into and reworking the narrative. Further, Margery's relationship to the infant (and infantilized) Christ is as his nursemaid. Some of the most powerful images of Margery constructing female communities and revising her birth experiences and history are located in these visions.[28]

Following Margery's meditation on Christ outlined above, Margery has a vision in which Christ instructs her to think about his mother, Mary, who is the "cause of alle þe grace þat þow hast."[29] Her immediate response is to think of Mary's mother, Anne, in a pregnant state. Like the opening chapter, the initial focus in this chapter (Chapter Six) is on the experience of pregnancy. Following shortly on the heels of her own experience of birth, this vision is also a way for Margery to relate her own painful birth experience to the more sacred, sanctioned, and (seemingly) painless births of Anne and Mary. Thus, Margery rewrites her own experience, reconnecting herself to the birth process as a mediator (midwife). Margery's account of Anne's and Mary's birth ignores any physical elements of their pregnancy and birth, any pain, illness, or fear they might have had. This kind of bodily elision is commonplace, and it is conventionally written into the narrative of the Virgin Mary, but not necessarily of that of her mother, Anne, or John the Baptist's mother Elizabeth, both of whom Margery "attends" in birth.

Margery's narrative isn't entirely devoid of recognition of the social performance of birth, nor is it entirely a reaffirmation of the maternal mythology of a Virgin or holy birth created from God's word and will. In fact, Margery places herself in the position of both midwife and Godlike intercessor, as a participant in, even re-creator of, Christian history, rather than just as a transmitter and imitator of it.[30] She achieves this through multiple involvements with the women she imagines herself attending. She immediately begins to imagine herself as the pregnant St. Anne's maid, and subsequently as Mary and Elizabeth's handmaiden. In pondering first Anne's pregnancy, then Mary's and Elizabeth's, our attention is drawn to the matrilineal, rather than the patrilineal, origin of Christ, a move that suggests Margery relates to the maternal community of Christ. This is not to say that Margery places creation in the hands of women, but rather that procreation, even as part of Christ's history, at least for Margery, is a communal female event. She draws these women and their experiences (holy sanctioned childbirth) together in the narrative in a single historical moment and reenacts them, reproducing them in the text. She is also the agent who brings these women together within the narrative, first in tending Anne in birth, then in bringing up Mary, and then in serving Mary and accompanying her to, and attending, Elizabeth in her birth of John the Baptist.

Many of the duties she performs were those done by midwives, including delivering and swaddling the infant, and caring for the mother's physical needs before, during, and after labor. Margery follows—sometimes symbolically, sometimes more literally—the basic elements of the birth rituals that were likely performed by birthing communities. Beginning with a metaphorical conception, the text then engages in a separation process, which is reminiscent of the structure of the lying-in room where all light is blocked out and where men are excluded and where the focus is on the mother-to-be (as described in Chapter One). There are elements of separation from and exclusion of the society of men through the construction of a female community (including ceremonial rituals such as preparing and drinking caudle, swaddling, and possibly baptism). There is then a transition back into the society of men, and then a full reintegration into everyday life through sanctioned ceremony (Purification or Churching). This "ritual" cycle takes place in the narrative beginning with Anne's pregnancy and ending with the visit of the three Kings to the Christ child.

The process begins with what I consider a metaphorical conception, when Christ suggests to Margery that she "thynke of my Modyr" (Mary). It is as if Christ, in answering to Kempe's "mende," has impregnated her with the idea of Mary; again, as above, Margery has supplied the matter, her mind and her willingness to meditate, and Christ has supplied the form, the thought. This image also resembles the Annunciation when the word becomes flesh, and Gabriel informs Mary that she will be the mother of Christ; here Christ is the messenger and Margery, Mary. Once Christ has done his work, however, Margery creates her own narrative where she plays a leading role. In casting herself as a significant figure, the narrative now becomes hers rather than Christ's. This she does to the exclusion of all men except Christ, and most notably in a chapter with so many births. The elision of paternity here is complex in specific relation to Margery's and the text's reproductive unconscious, for Margery plays maternal and paternal roles as well.

Once Margery begins her contemplation of Mary, she becomes immersed in mothers. When she "thinks on Mary," she immediately focuses not on Mary as Christ's mother, but rather on Mary's mother Anne when she was "gret wyth chylde." Margery creates a matrilineal narrative, focusing initially on the pregnant mother as happens in the narrative of herself in the opening chapters. In attending Anne as her "mayden & hir seruawnt," Margery becomes involved in all aspects of Anne's pregnancy and birth. But Anne's actual birth experience is elided. Instead of the long, painful and illness-ridden pregnancy and birth that Margery experiences in the first chapter, Anne delivers without much ado—the experience is described as "& anon ower Lady was born." Margery then puts herself in the role of the mother, again in contrast to her own pregnancy; the care of Mary seems to fall primarily on her: "ʒan sche besyde hir to take þe chyld to hir & kepe it tyl it wer twelve ʒer of age wyth good mete & drynke, wyth fayr whyte clothys & whyte kerchys."[31] In this passage she is beside Anne, attending her to "take the child to her and keep it until it was twelve years of age." Margery is described as tending to the very material aspects of parenting—food and clothing—"good food and drink, and with fair white clothes and white kerchiefs."[32] The whiteness of Mary's clothes is traditional Virgin attire, and one cannot help but notice that this image is repeated several times in the text in relation both to Mary and Margery, showing Margery's own desire for Virginal—and perhaps maternal and mediatrix—status.[33]

Margery extends her parenting of Mary beyond earthly maternity and into the "ghostly," for she places herself as the messenger angel in announcing to Mary, "Lady, þe schal be þe Modyr of God," effectively placing herself as Gabriel, as well as the Father of God and the Creator, rather than the procreator.[34] Margery then becomes alienated from the sacred birth plot; she is not involved in Mary's pregnancy in the same way she is in St. Anne's and Elizabeth's. Margery's lack of involvement is complicated by the fact that Margery's voice is always in question. Her transcriber, himself an intercessor of the word of God, as well as the words of Margery Kempe, might seek occlusion of Margery's role in Mary's pregnancy to deny her the creative power that Margery seems to be insisting on in other places in the narrative.

Further, it is not clear whether Mary's removal from the bodily experience of pregnancy, in addition to following the narrative of the Virgin birth, results from the scribe's or Margery's discomfort with the birth experience. For example, Mary is not described as being pregnant in the same way as her mother, Anne, is (which itself is minimal); instead she is described as going away and then coming back and announcing that she is now the Mother of God: "The blysful chyld passyd awey for a certyn tyme, þe cratur being stylle in contemplacyon, and sythen cam a-gyn and seyd, 'Dowtyr, now am I be-kome þe Modyr of God.'"[35] In fact, she has not actually given birth at this point (although this is not entirely clear until later when Mary does finally give birth). This confusion in the texts suggests that there is no way to tell when one can accurately be described as having become a mother. In fact, Mary here is described as a "blissful child" as opposed to a pregnant woman, suggesting her own youthfulness and the trope of innocence, rather than maternity.[36] This is also a way for the text to infantilize Mary, denying her anything but a passive role, if even that, in Christ's birth.[37] Mary's case also replicates contemporary theories on women's roles in reproduction: she is literally the vessel for God's—or in this case Margery's—word, or form. In addition, her passing away "for a certain time" suggests a real disassociation from (and perhaps ignorance of), as well as an anxiety over, the birth process. Mary simply disappears for an undisclosed period, while Margery continues her meditation. The whole of a woman's reproductive process occurs outside the realm of the written, except in the realm of medical texts, and is therefore in the realm of the unknown.

Even while the text expresses a distance from, and perhaps a distaste for, the knowledge and process of birth and female reproduction, it also reveals specific elements of the childbirth ritual in the course of the description of Elizabeth's birth of St. John the Baptist and Mary's birth of Christ. These ceremonial elements suggest how the female community was brought together within the childbirth ritual. To begin, Margery brings with her to Elizabeth a "potel of pyment & spycys ʒerto."[38] This bottle of sweetened spiced wine conjures up the image of the caudle served to laboring and recently delivered women by their midwives and assistants—better known as gossips.[39] It makes perfect sense that Margery would be carrying the traditional caudle given the proximity and nature of the events in her narrative; they are on their way to a pregnant Elizabeth, where they "wonyd to-gedyr" for twelve weeks. These kinds of gatherings before the birth were known as gossipings. That is, Margery and Mary function essentially as gossips (and midwives) to Elizabeth, living with her and attending her until the birth of her child.

The text then outlines several important elements of the role of a midwife while also revealing some interesting notions about women and reproduction. When Elizabeth is delivered of John the Baptist, "owyr Lady toke hym vp fro þe erthe wyth al maner reuerns & ȝaf hym to hys moder, syeng of hym þat he scheld be an holy man, and blyssed hym."⁴⁰ First, Mary seems to hold the honored position of midwife in that she presents Elizabeth with her son. Mary also holds an honored position in that she reveals sacred knowledge—that "he shall be a holy man." In addition, Mary blesses John the Baptist. However, Mary does not deliver the infant from Elizabeth's womb, but rather takes "hym vp fro þe erthe," which glosses over Elizabeth's physical experience of birth, and suggests her alienation from John the Baptist's creation in that he comes from the ground. This suggests he was perhaps made by God, rather than woman, but it also reminds us of the sins of body, even in a sanctioned and sacred, though not virginal, birth such as Elizabeth's.

When Mary gives birth, the birth ritual becomes even more suggestive of the power of the female community. In addition, the text shows Margery as further rewriting her idyllic birth experience through her participation in Mary's birth, and consequently revises biblical history. Mary's birth of Christ also dramatizes the common understanding of the Virgin Birth, which is without pain and, presumably, any physical ailment or complication. While there are images of the midwife's role in Mary's birth, there is a real absence of a physical description of labor. The standard narrative of Mary's birth of Jesus leaves out pain and midwives, but with Joseph on hand (although not necessarily at the birth itself). Interestingly, while Margery's narrative of Mary's childbirth experience follows the painless, laborless scenario, it excludes Joseph entirely, and includes Margery as midwife.⁴¹ The usual narrative of Mary, which includes a doubting and somewhat troubled Joseph, is abandoned for a matrilineal narrative which enacts the exclusion of men and functions as a metaphorical "sealing off" or enclosure like a lying-in chamber itself. For example, there is no mention of Joseph until Mary, Margery, and Joseph commence their journey to attend a pregnant Elizabeth, at which point we learn nothing whatsoever of Joseph's role, and much about Margery's and Mary's.

Margery, who assists Mary in Elizabeth's labor, takes the role of midwife in Mary's labor. In fact, she also takes on the role of Joseph in terms of caring for Mary before the birth. Margery "purchasyd hir herborwe euery night wyth gret reuerens, & owyr Lady was receyued wyth glad cher"—she plays the role of Joseph by arranging for Mary's lodgings, or "purchasing her harbor."⁴² Margery also prepares for the upcoming birth by begging for the same kinds of garments to swaddle the infant Jesus in as she dressed the child Mary in: "Also sche beggyd owyr Lady fayr whyte clothys & kerchy for to swathyn in hir Sone whan he wer born."⁴³ There is an element of maternal continuity in this image, and the expectation that Margery will not only assist in the birth, but act as midwife in it (swaddling the infant was one of the key honors of attending a birth). Finally, suggesting the practice and the order of birth rituals are the images of baptism, when

Margery "ordeyned beddyng for owyr Lady to lyg in wyth hir blyssed Sone."⁴⁴ In preparing the bedding for Mary and her infant to lie in, Margery performs a kind of baptism in "swaddling" Christ with "byttyr teerys of compassyon, hauyng mend of þe scharp deth þat he schuld suffyr for þe lofe of synful men." Her swaddling with tears is both a symbolic baptism and a prefiguration of Mary's and others' own sorrow at her son's death.⁴⁵

Margery succeeds in setting up a narrative in which a female community can produce a child without men, rewriting history as well. This representation of female management and production is Margery's symbolic act of procreation and of female creation. It is in keeping with the paradigm of birth rituals that Margery constructs this act. Margery's meditation ends with the reintegration of Mary (and Margery as well) to the company of men as signaled by the visit of the Three Kings to Mary, the return of Joseph to the narrative, and the return of Christ as a director of Margery's thoughts. This symbolic "reintegration" of men back into the text, men who hold at times titular roles (as in the case of the Three Kings and Joseph), further suggests that the whole birth process, even to some degree conception, can happen very well without the participation of men.⁴⁶

Margery Kempe and the Worshipful Wives

Margery's figuration of female communities in her meditation on Mary reaches idyllic levels, yet her social experiences fall short of this. Especially compelling in its representation of female communities, and giving several views of a reproductive unconscious, is the Christ doll incident. In this incident, Margery socially performs with other women some of the sacred maternal practices of her meditation. Just as she cared for the Christ child in her vision, Margery shares in a recurring ritual adoration of an image of Christ. In so doing, Margery's *Book* also brings together and represents in a poignant way female textual, devotional, and birth communities.

While Margery is traveling with a group of people (including two friars and her Irish companion, Richard) on her pilgrimage from Jerusalem to Rome, she participates in a ritual—and it is presented as a ritual, that is, as something that occurs on a regular basis—that brings together a group of women for devotional purposes. In fact, the ritual is particularly representational of female textual, birth, and devotional communities, suggesting several different social and cultural performances that are not normally available to us. Margery participates in this ritual with a woman who "bar a chyst & an ymage þerin mad aftyr our Lord," an image of Christ in the form of a doll:

> And þe woman the which had þe ymage in þe chist, whan þei comyn in good citeys, sche toke owt þe ymage owt of hir chist & sett it in worshepful wyfys lappys. & þei wold puttyn schirtys þerup-on & kyssyn it as þei it had ben God hym-selfe.⁴⁷

A Very Maternal Mysticism: Images of Childbirth and Its Rituals

First, the woman carries the image of Christ with her in a chest from city to city, and in each "good" city she comes with her chest containing the image of Christ and places it on "worshipful wives' laps." The wives then dress the Christ doll and kiss it "as if it had been God Himself." The group of women function within the narrative as a representation of a spiritual and devotional (female) community, revering and worshiping Christ through the medium of a doll.[48] That these women dress and kiss the Christ doll while holding it in their laps and while passing it from woman to woman—worshipful wife to worshipful wife—shows that this shared ritual is more than just typical devotional behavior. Gail McMurray Gibson has argued that the placing of the Christ doll in the wives' laps is "a ritual blessing of the womb to ensure fruitfulness and protection from the dangers of childbirth as much as opportunity for visual contemplation of the Nativity of Christ."[49] I would suggest further that this performance is also "textual."

In one reading, the chest and Christ doll can be seen as a text whose content is shared among a group of women (as it is passed from lap to lap) in the manner a textual community might share a text. The passing of the doll replicates dissemination of knowledge, where the doll as the image of Christ is not the agent, but rather the text to be shared, as a passive article to be "read." The dressing of the Christ doll further emphasizes the inertness of the image, placing the interpretation, the dressing, literally in the hands of the women who receive it.[50] Each woman can dress or undress the Christ doll, the "text," in the manner she desires. They have the power to manipulate, to read, the image in their own terms. The women could read and worship the Christ doll as the symbolic sacred infant; they might also see the doll as their own infant and a chance to practice maternity, to "play with dolls"; they may also see this as an opportunity, like Margery in earlier chapters, to rewrite their own reproductive history.

Another reading suggests that this gathering reveals some elements of female participation in birth events such as gossiping and childbirth, both of which bring to mind the notion of women disseminating knowledge through gossips. The participants, and in particular Margery, together undertake to attend the Virgin Mary symbolically through the care and caressing of her infant Jesus doll. For Margery, the image of these women rehearsing Christ's birth as they attend to the infant doll provokes the memory of images of the birth and childhood of Christ she had had when she was back in England:

> ...& sche was meuyd in so mych þe mor as, whil sche was in Inglond, sche had hy meditacyons in þe byrth & þe childhode of Crist, & sche thankyd God for-as-mech as sche saw þes creaturys han so gret feyth in þat sche sey wyth hir bodily eye lych as sche had be-forn wyth hir gostly eye.[51]

Margery is described as "so much the more moved" by these women because "she saw these creatures had as great faith in that she saw with her bodily eye as she had before with her ghostly eye." Margery is unified with these women by an event, Christ's birth, and its subsequent reenactment. The text here places the ritual of these women coddling and kissing the Christ doll as akin to the real birth and childhood of Christ, that which "sche sey wyth hir bodily eye," as compared to Margery's rehearsal of the event, that which she saw with her "ghostly eye." Yet the doll remains symbolic, and the adoration of it, while creating a female community that Margery can participate in, still falls short of the ideal virginal role.

This rehearsal and remembrance of Christ's birth in the Christ doll is another opportunity for Margery to rewrite her reproductive history through participating in and constructing a female sacred birth community, and through a metaphoric enactment of birth. In keeping with the idea of the physical manifestation and production of the symbolic Christ-child, Margery becomes the mother, Mary, and seems to act out the throes of childbirth: "whan þes good women seyn þis creatur wepyn, sobbyn, & creyn so wondirfully & mythtyly þat sche was nerhand ouyrcomyn þerwyth."[52] Margery, in response to seeing the women's worship of the doll, begins sobbing "so wonderfully and mightily that she was nearly overcome therewith," an image which suggests a physical rapture similar to labor. This passage, in conjunction with the passages quoted above, echoes the birth ritual where the act of the women coming together suggests the gossips who attend a birth; the doll, which is held in their laps, suggests the infant in childbirth, and the dressing and kissing of the doll suggests the swaddling. The text also marks Margery as the mother (as opposed to the woman metaphorically described as a pregnant woman: "whech bar a chest & an ymage þerin"), who weeps, sobs, and loudly cries out in a rehearsal of birth and delivery.

The concluding moment of this passage and the chapter also suggests the event of childbirth. The other women place Margery, as she herself placed Mary and Jesus after Mary's delivery, on a bed. The language used to describe Margery in her assistance of Mary is the same language used in describing how the worshipful wives help Margery. Margery "ordeyned beddyng for owyr Lady to lyg in wyth hir blyssed Sone,"[53] while the women "ordeyned a good soft bed & leyd hir þerup-on & comfortyd hir as mech as þei myth for ouyr Lordys lofe, blyssed mot he ben.[54] As is true of the earlier passage, an element and image of baptism appears in the "ordaining" of a "good soft bed." This time, however, the recipient is Margery, where she once again is conflated with the Virgin Mary. As Kathy Lavezzo points out, this ritual functions on one level as a means for the women to express their "identification with and desire for...the Virgin Mary."[55] I would add that in the case of Margery, it is a specific desire to be Mary and a means of rewriting her own reproductive history. This is another opportunity for Margery to reenact her own labor, and, by doing so in terms of Christ's birth, Margery somehow "atones for...the sin of female sexuality, which

A Very Maternal Mysticism: Images of Childbirth and Its Rituals 57

labor in childbirth punishes," thereby fulfilling the needs of the culture.[56] But, according to models suggested by *Hali Meidenhad* and the *Ancrene Wisse*, to truly atone for her sins as Julian seeks to, Margery would have to abandon these social interactions.

On the other hand, to place oneself (or to be placed) in the position of enacting Mary is still to enact the patristic notions of idealized female behavior. While the Christ doll passage suggests the power of female procreation in its symbolic force as a ritual of birth, it also suggests further elision of female procreative force in that the infant is an inert doll, and the wives are only able to "play" with the doll, not actually mother it. In addition, the male transcriber (along with potentially any number of other males) is made privy to it. That men have access to this ritual both reveals its power as well as deflates it. The ritual is made "safe" because it is viewable, out in the open. It also shows women gathered together around the "infant" in scripted action; in the case of gossipings, women are not scripted, and there is no male control. This shows the reproductive unconscious in that the text attempts to take the mystery out of a metaphorical gossiping by representing it as an ideal gathering of women (gossips).

THE REPRODUCTIVE UNCONSCIOUS AND THE AMANUENSIS

The problematic nature of the *Book*'s production raises questions about the representations of Margery's lived and visionary experience, and adds an interesting dimension to the theme of male intercessor and intruder. While the *Book* is often cited as the first surviving English autobiography, the work comes to us through an amanuensis;[57] it is "dictated" by Margery to a priest.[58] Whether Margery was in fact illiterate or literate is not known. Even as she claims herself to be "illiterate" and is accepted as such by most scholars, Margery exerts a certain level of authority over her text.[59] And, as Karma Lochrie has shown us, "medieval mystical texts...depart from this [written] tradition of authorization" in that mystic discourse traditionally originates from or privileges the oral.[60] In any case, the fact that there is clearly a male intercessor suggests that this text is "dialogic in a startlingly literal sense."[61] That is to say, in this text, the "voice" of Margery is intertwined with the patriarchal ideology of her transcriber—leaving areas for interpretation of two voices. The dialogic nature of the text raises several questions and difficulties in reading the *Book* as a uniquely female autobiography that might give us insights into the uniquely female experiences of pregnancy and childbirth. In addition, despite her exercising "authority" over the text, it is hard to know for certain to what extent Margery Kempe controlled the structure and content of the narrative.[62] Kempe's *Book*, particularly in light of its problematic "authorship," suggests views of the reproductive unconscious from varying cultural locations. So, the medieval notions of maternity and virginity that are behind the repressions are conceived of (so to speak) from various subject positions. For example, the

Priest to whom Margery dictated her *Book* would likely have had a particular comprehension, both spiritually and physically, of celibacy. As well, he would have had something at stake in portraying Margery's own struggle for celibacy as a means to attaining holiness. Margery's celibacy, on the other hand, may have come as much from her desire to be rid of sexual obligations to her husband and the duties of bearing children as it was a means of expressing her devotion to Christ and God. (It so happens that one does get "released" from certain duties as a mystic, whether enclosed, as Julian was, or not.) Further, Margery's Priest's experience of childbirth and its rituals was likely to have been limited to whatever ceremonial functions he performed; he would not have attended or participated in a birth, nor would he have had firsthand experience with the rituals performed in the lying-in space. He would, however, have been well acquainted with biblical nativities. Margery, on the other hand, had a very intimate knowledge of the experience (fourteen experiences, to be precise), and it seems likely that she would parlay these into her spiritual visions which would be a location that would be common to both the Priest and Margery.

Delectable and Devout Ghostly and Earthly Sights

Margery's response to other women (and their midwives) and Mary on Purification Day highlights the issue of the male intruder and the potential role of the amanuenses' conflicted view of Margery and the communities that get figured in her visions. When Margery experiences the physical presence of an infant, doll, or recently delivered mother, she imagines Mary and Christ's infancy, childhood, or passion.[63] In addition, she is reminded of her own maternity and relationship to her children, a memory that seems to cause discomfort; she immediately turns to the visionary. Just as the sight of and participation in the ritual of tending to the Christ doll inspires and reminds Margery of Christ and his childhood, the witnessing of women undergoing the Purification ritual after childbirth reminds Margery of Mary's Purification after Christ's birth:

> She had swech holy thowtys & meditacyons many tyme whan sche saw women ben purifyid of her childeryn. Sche thowt in hir sowle þat sche saw owr Lady ben purifijd & had hy contemplacyon in þe beheldyng of þe women wheche comyn to offeryn wyth þe women þat weryn purifijd.[64]

Margery conflates the recently delivered women with Mary, and she reveres these as she does the Virgin Mary—a kind of flip side of the reverence and attention the worshipful wives accorded Margery in the passage above. The attention and focus here is on the women themselves, and it is the ritual of Purification that is the catalyst for Margery's "ghostly" vision. Like the physical rituals themselves, the ghostly sights are accompanied by physical elements, most often with weeping and crying, that suggest pregnancy and childbirth.

A Very Maternal Mysticism: Images of Childbirth and Its Rituals 59

By imagining an intimate exchange over group dissemination, and by linking this kind of devotion to a pleasurable experience using images of birth and barrenness, Margery's *Book* demonstrates the power of reproductive discourse. Specifically, while the Purification ritual suggests Margery's strong attachment to female devotional and childbirth communities, it also leads into a description that suggests Margery's alienation from these same groups, marking them as inadequate. Purification is the part of the ritual of childbirth that men were most involved in and in which the Church actively played a role (in addition to baptism). In the Purification day scene, we are reminded again of the directive and prime role of God and Christ in women's reproductive duties. Patriarchal ideology desires not groups of women gossips—which lead to the classic coupling of sexuality with verbosity and the classic male anxiety over the inevitable unbridled language and sexuality that comes with it—but rather desires contained, enclosed women who remain virgins and intact and whose language remains in check.[65] Thus, the text involves itself in the containment of the women. Instead of building a community, such as Margery achieves earlier, this incident seeks to break down that community by instilling in women an anxiety about their behavior in relation to other women.[66]

As opposed to the passage quoted earlier in which Kempe appropriates Christ's suggestion and writes her own narrative, this passage shows Margery as abject and inert in anticipation of God's thoughts. She not only expresses her desires to be the passive vessel (as in many previous passages), but she acts on these desires as well (instead of against them as in earlier passages). For one thing, the language used to describe her experience is closely bound up with the language of material or "earthly" reproduction, where Margery's tears, or lack thereof, become a metaphor for fertility and barrenness respectively:

> Sche had þes myndys & þes desyrys wyth profownded teerys, syhyngys, & sobbyngys, & sumtyme wyth gret boistowsness cryingys as God wolde sende it, & sumtyme softe teerys and preuy wyth-owtyn any boistowesnesse.[67]

Margery ruminates on the thoughts that Christ gives privately and specifically to her, thoughts that yield physical rapture, which she expresses through her trademark affective (and abject) crying: "She had these minds (thoughts) and desires with profound tears, sighings and sobbings, and sometimes with great boisterousness (violent cryings)." This passage also emphasizes the very intimate nature of the experience; God sends his thoughts "sometimes with soft and privy tears without any roughness." God has control over what she receives, and we understand these thoughts as "privy" in the sense that she both cries privately, and that what God (or Christ) sends her is "private."

In this particular case, the presence of God and Christ in Margery's mind are directly associated with the onset of crying and of fertility. Conversely, the absence of God and Christ are associated with a lack of tears and barrenness, where the "privity" of God and woman is once again posited in relation to procreation:

> Sche myth ney er wepyn lowde ne stille but what God wolde sende it hir, for sche was sumtyme so bareyn fro teerys a day er sumtyme half a day & had so gret peyne for desyr þat sche had of hem þat sche wold a ȝouyn al þis worlde, yt it had ben hir, for a fewe terrys, þer a suffyrd ryth gret bodily peyne for to a gotyn hem wyth. And þan, whan sche was so bareyn, sche cowde fynde no joye ne no comforte in mete ne drynke.[68]

She is so barren of tears, and in such great pain in her desire to have them, she would have done anything "for a few tears, or suffered great bodily pain to have got with them." The phrase suggests that Margery would have suffered a great deal to obtain them, and also—as women in childbirth do—to have "got with them," for to lack tears is to be barren, infertile. By associating tears with the image of fertility and pregnancy, and the lack of tears with infertility and barrenness, the text attempts to make Margery's metaphorical experience of her own maternity more notable on a physical—that is procreative—and material level, rather than on the imaginative and creative level seen earlier.[69]

As earlier, the ideal solution is for Margery to meditate and receive God's images passively, and to remove herself from the realm of the social family community to the realm of the spiritual community. And, as in Julian's case, the culture demands male mediation of her devotions. Unlike Julian, however, Margery does not fit readily into either the enclosed, physically transcendent location that Julian inhabits, neither does she find respite in earthly familial relationships. Just as she is accused of and shows some Lollard tendencies in her *Book*, it is almost as if her sexual and spiritual struggle is towards an as yet non-existent married chastity.

CHAPTER FOUR

"with grievous groanes & deepe sighes"
Female Textual and Birth Communities in *The Monument of Matrones*

When Joan Kelly first asked the question "Did women have a Renaissance?" in her famous essay of the same title, she might not have imagined how frequently and in how many different ways scholars after her would ask the same question.[1] I want to continue to ask the question in terms of how things changed for women in early modern England in specific relation to their roles as mothers, midwives, and gossips, and specifically as Protestant mothers, midwives, and gossips. The text that I examine in this chapter is one that reveals these changes and is one that few scholars address: the late sixteenth-century collection *The Monument of Matrones*, compiled and edited by Thomas Bentley in 1582.[2] The text contains devotions, meditations, and prayers that either take up the subject of childbirth explicitly, as in the case of the childbirth prayers in Lamp Five, or implicitly, as in the use of reproductive metaphors in describing the production of the text. Thus, I assert that this text, like its medieval predecessors, shows how early modern men and women negotiated a conflict between the ideological and material need of the culture for them to procreate, and an ideological injunction that they remain chaste. However, the terms of chastity shift through the course of the Reformation. Instead of the enclosed celibacy offered in *Ancrene Wisse*, Julian of Norwich's *Book of Showings*, and *The Book of Margery Kempe*, *Monument* offers examples of married chastity—it addresses and gives exemplars of all manner of women, but particularly married women. In addition to a different model of virginity, *Monument* also expresses different values for childbirth through its representations of them. The prayers show a very close relationship to devotional practices: while devotional texts in the middle ages used images of childbirth to describe spiritual states and insights, the early modern *Monument* inverts this relationship, using sacred images at times to sanctify childbirth itself. This text brings the women's own acts of childbirth directly into the devotions and thereby both privileges childbirth as sacred to God and attempts to relocate these acts within a sacred structure that is also masculine.

Monument also suggests the different ways maternity and the role of the mother get envisioned in Reformation England. As opposed to the view of motherhood offered in *Hali Meidenhad*, in which marriage and motherhood are *much* less desirable than virginity, *Monument* presents motherhood as having greater importance than in the middle ages. However, these representations are still mediated through a male editor. As in my discussions of medieval texts, I posit the idea of a reproductive unconscious in order to think about the conflict between the dominant culture's ideas of maternity and female subversion of those ideas. In *Monument* I examine how the reproductive unconscious in this text emerges in multiple "voices" or reproductive narratives that complicate our notions of women's authority as patrons, queens, and mothers—narratives that also show women's changing relationship to God, Christ, and the Virgin Mary. I also demonstrate how these texts challenge and extend our ideas about the childbirth scene, the birth ritual, and female textual communities by giving further insights into the culture's changing notions of maternal duty.

The layout and general contents of *Monument* have significant cultural implications for female textual and birth communities. As one of the earliest, and, indeed, largest devotional works compiled and published specifically for women, *Monument* offers modern scholars an example of how female textual communities were imagined and how female devotional practices were articulated. Examining the prayers, devotions, and meditations written by and for women in *Monument* can help us to reconstruct and get a sense of the status and experiences of sixteenth-century women (as much as it is possible to retrieve and reconstruct any history of this kind). The text is remarkable because it includes voices and works by women who were crucial to the Reformation, women such as Katherine Parr, Anne Askew, Queen Elizabeth, and Marguerite de Navarre. These women not only could stand as examples of Godly women, but they also helped define and create a "location" for private female devotion.

Monument contains more than a thousand pages, divided up into seven "Lamps" or sections, that contain works by or for women. Each "Lamp of Virginity," as the text's subtitle refers to them, appears to be designed for use in a series of situations. Lamp One is a collection of biblical excerpts, "divine praiers, hymns, of songs made by sundrie holie women in the scripture"; and Lamp Seven contains the "acts & histories, lives & deaths of all maner of women, good and bad, mentioned in the holy scripture," appearing in alphabetical order.[3] These two lamps place the devotional material of Lamps Two through Six in a context of women in biblical history, their prayers occupying the first lamp, their lives the last. Lamp Two contains prayers and meditations of women such as Lady Jane Dudley, Marguerite de Navarre, and Katherine Parr. Lamp Three contains prayers and divine meditations "penned by the godlie learned, to be properlie used of the Queene's most excellent Maiestie," with particular emphasis on the anniversary of her ascension. The Fourth Lamp is made up of prayers and meditations for use at various "principall feasts, daies, houres, times, and seasons of the yeere, privatlie." Lamp Five, which is the focus of this chapter, addresses the various stages and offices of women's lives, including maids, wives, mothers, mistresses and servants, and widows. Lamp Six appears to be a directory, a "mirror for Maidens and Matrons," which describes the appropriate Godly vocations, and includes stories of various Godly women. Each Lamp appears self-contained with its own "title" page and sometimes its own set of page numbers, suggesting that the text might have been intended for publication originally in pamphlets or in installments. The first lamp, for example, is numbered pages 1–49, and Lamp Five also has its own set of page numbers, 1–212. In addition, while not as portable as, say, Katherine Parr's very popular octavo edition of *Prayers or Meditations* (which is reprinted in *Monument*), the quarto texts would be both portable and presumably more affordable than the whole. A distinguishing factor of Lamp Five in particular is the inclusion of a table of prayers in the form of five final leaves, which essentially act as a table of contents. If Lamp Five was published as a separate pamphlet, as its composition suggests, its size and content would make it quite suitable for private use in a house, chamber, or birthing area by one or several women.

Approximately thirty-eight of the one hundred fifteen prayers in Lamp Five are related to the subject of childbirth; some of these are specifically intended for the pregnant, laboring, or recently delivered mother, some specifically for the midwife. Of these, the prayers vary in tone and intensity. While most all of the prayers seem to ask God for less painful contractions, some focus quite explicitly on the physical experience of birth, as well as the intense pain, anguish, and anxiety over a safe delivery. Because the prayers are of unknown authorship, it is unclear whether or not those that express an unusual empathy with the laboring woman are indeed written by women, or if they are an indication of a male author's familiarity with the female experience of birth. Similarly, it is impossible to know if the prayers that express a difficult relationship between the speaker and the reproductive female body derive from a male voice penetrating a female experience, or a female voice echoing the male or female discomfort with women's birthing bodies. In either case, all the prayers are filtered through a man, because they are both compiled and edited by one. As in the case of Margery Kempe's *Book*, which contains a female voice filtered through a male amanuensis, these mediations allow us the potential for multiple views of the reproductive unconscious. The "voice" of the text is complicated by the presence of the prayers and meditations that project a female voice, addressing the female experience of birth, and the editorial work of Thomas Bentley that projects a male, patriarchal subjectivity.

I analyze these prayers, then, not as unmediated expressions of what happens during the childbirth ritual, but rather as a complex expression of both patriarchal and maternal desires and fears of what happens during the ritual. The childbirth prayers in *Monument* show the complexity of the early modern maternal experience, setting up certain traditional models and expectations of appropriate, decidedly unprivileged, maternal behavior, while at the same time suggesting that the woman's role in childbirth is a privileged one, particularly in relationship to God and Christ. Theorizing a reproductive unconscious in analyzing the childbirth prayers sheds light on changing complex expectations and roles of the mother, gossip, and attendant in the childbirth scene because of the changes in the configuration of that unconscious.

Medieval to Early Modern Childbirth, Devotional, and Literacy Practices

Women's practices of devotion, literacy, childbirth and maternity were tied to the changing and shifting ideologies and discourses. For example, medical views of women remained essentially unchanged from antiquity until the late-seventeenth and early-eighteenth centuries. However, the advent of the printing press changed other elements of the female birth experience and ritual. Early modern midwifery manuals, exclusively male-authored until Jane Sharp's *The Midwives Book* published in 1671, became widely available and likely used by women in the mid-sixteenth century and onward.[4] The most popular manual was Thomas Raynald's *The Byrth of Mankynde*, translated from Rösslin's *De partu hominius*, which went through approximately thirteen editions beginning in 1540, in addition to the later Jacques Guillemeau's *Child-Birth, or the Happy Deliverie of Women* (1612). These male-authored texts, particularly *Byrth*, worked, whether consciously or unconsciously, to instill a fear in the pregnant woman about the competence of her midwife, in turn creating an even more fearful experience of maternity for women. In addition, the translator of *Byrth* suggests that his work reveals women's secrets for all to read.[5] In the process of claiming privy knowledge of women's bodies and reproductive practices, *Byrth* and similar texts imagined themselves infiltrating a previously exclusively female occupation and experience. The appearance of texts like these accompanied a gradual movement of male-midwives and physicians into the female birth ritual.[6]

Women nonetheless were responsible for taking care of the health of their families, households, and communities, depending on their social status; these practices offer an example of the type of "textual" community that may well have educated the midwife and potential birth attendants.[7] Female health practitioners were especially prevalent in rural villages and country estates where physicians would have to come quite a long way to treat sick patients and where treatment by physicians would be costly. The medical profession excluded women both from authorized and unauthorized practice in several different ways: most textbooks and medical manuals were written in Latin, a language that most women were not taught to read, and formal academic and specifically medical education was limited to men. For the most part, women learned about herbs, remedies, childbirth, menstruation, pregnancy, delivery, menopause, anatomy and physiology, and other everyday elements of health care from other women. These women ostensibly transferred information from one to another through word-of-mouth, apprenticeships, diaries, private (and a very few published) medical handbooks, and midwives' books.[8] As Lady Grace Mildmay's medical papers suggest, women may have written their own versions of medical handbooks and textbooks for various medical needs, including childbirth practices, which they shared with each other, but for which there is very little evidence. For example, while there were a very few medical writings in English or translated into English, texts containing recipes for herbal remedies were "standard household possessions."[9] For the most part, these books were not published, but like many medieval and early modern works they would have circulated in manuscript form.

While the experience of physical pain and anxiety connected with childbirth remains constantly identifiable in both medieval and early modern texts, the expression of this experience changed over the course of pre-Reformation and Reformation England. This is in part because the nature of devotional practices was evolving, especially for women, and this, in turn, affected the manner in which the woman's body was mediated. Specifically, devotional practices of pre-Reformation England, on the one hand, emphasized and focused on the physicality of Christ's birth, passion, crucifixion, and resurrection, casting Mary as the Mediatrix. On the other hand, Reformation conventions of meditational and devotional practices came out of a Protestant theology that sought not to dwell on the bodily events of Christ's life, but rather redirected a devotional focus on the written Word of God. Some scholars have argued that the Protestant model of private devotion was a more "congenial" way for women to address and approach God without the male intermediary of the Catholic Priest.[10] While Protestant devotional practices privileged the written word and promoted individual meditations, private contemplation was not entirely a liberating one for women. In some ways, Reformation and Protestant models of devotion were more restrictive than the discourses of devotion available to medieval women, in part because the Virgin Mary was worshipped with less zealousness than she had been in late medieval and early sixteenth-century England, and in part because the terms of devotion were redirected to the written word and the self.[11] In pre-Reformation England, anxieties and concerns about maternity and the potentially reproductive female body often made themselves known through representations of the Virgin Mary, the figure of perfect female behavior and maternal devotion. The materiality of Christ's and Mary's life were locations for the displacement of specifically bodily anxieties, fears, and desires onto sacred and sanctified images. Margery Kempe in her *Book* meditates heavily on Christ's and Mary's body in relation to her representations of female devotional communities; later works more often take up these images literally rather than metaphorically.[12] Further, Christ's body was also a location where these same images could be subverted. While there remained Catholics in post-Reformation England and under Mary's rule, the evidence suggests that the intense affinity with the bodily experience of the birth and life of Christ and Mary was more muted in this period.

Protestant ideology put a great deal of emphasis on literacy, or more specifically the ability to read and less often write in the vernacular. Medieval and Early Modern English women's written work was initially limited to religious discourse of devotional writings and translations. In the later sixteenth century, however, women expanded their repertoire to include writings to their children, mother's advice books, such as Elizabeth Grymeston's *Miscelanea, Meditations, Memoratives* (1604). In the seventeenth century, autobiographies by such women as Margaret Cavendish, Alice Thornton, and Lucy Hutchinson were sometimes attached to their husband's autobiographies. Through their written discourses of meditations, devotionals, advice books, and "letters" to their children, early modern women had broader avenues than their medieval counterparts with which to express specifically female concerns and experiences of motherhood, maternal mortality, pregnancy, labor, childbirth, and infant mortality—even if they did not all address these issues equally explicitly.

BENTLEY'S FRAMING OF THE TEXT

Bentley imagines textual and devotional communities in *Monument* through the images and representations found on the title page, the Epistle and address to "the Christian Reader," and the texts he chooses for this compendium of virtue—in particular by the kinds of devotions, meditations, and prayers he includes. Bentley also imagines the ways female birth communities are constructed by the kinds of prayers and texts he includes that relate or refer to birth and birth communities, many of which appear in Lamp Five. In imagining these communities, he to some degree participates in constructing them as well. The three—devotional, textual, and birth communities—are interrelated in this, as in other texts. In this compilation of works, Bentley expresses his and the culture's desire for women to be chaste (as in married chastity), silent, contained, and obedient. At the same time, however, he praises, represents, and encourages women to be intelligent, inspirational, diligent, and productive (not just reproductive, although the text suggests that, too). Bentley, then, portrays the literary communities of women, whose works make up this text, in somewhat contradictory terms.

These conflicts can be seen, and are even epitomized, in the opening epithet that appears on the front page of *Monument*, "Let your loines be girt about, and your lampes burn clearly." In addition to referring to the ideal Christian behavior of women as "chaste, silent and obedient," this epithet represents ways the text in general is at odds with the way it imagines women and their devotional (and other) practices. The first line from the parable of the wise and foolish virgins (Luke 12:35–48), in which Christ tells of servants on watch for their master, reminds readers generally, and women specifically, that they must be faithful "servants" at all times; they should behave accordingly, and they must be prepared for Christ's arrival, whenever that might be.[13] (The idea that women are to men as good Christian men are to God was a common Christian paradigm.) A close reading of the quotation suggests both a certain respect and recognition of women and a desire to confine them. According to the *OED*, the verb "girt" is the past participle form of the verb "gird," which means "to surround, encircle (the waist, a person about the waist) with a belt or girdle, especially for the purpose of confining the garments and allowing freer action to the body" (s.v. "girt," def.1); the use of "gird" in "to gird one's loins" also has a biblical history, as seen be its frequent use throughout the Bible.[14] The literal meaning of "girt" is to surround with a belt or girdle for the purpose of gathering up garments for a "freer action of the body." But in freeing the legs, there is a restriction of the action of another part of the body, particularly the reproductive part of the female body—the loins are "the seats of physical strength and of generative power" ("loins," n. def 3). Restricting the seat of generative power suggests the desired image of an obedient and chaste female.

On the other hand, while one reading suggests that the loins of the women addressed should be covered, another reading might emphasize that their lamps should "burn clearly." The "lamp" can refer to, according to the *OED*, the "lamps" of "beauty, joy, life, etc.," ("lamp" n. def. 2c) frequently mentioned in biblical passages. But the Bible also uses the term lamp symbolically, relating the lamp used as "temple furniture" (that is, a candle holder) to wisdom (n. "lamp" def. 3).[15] A lamp, like a woman's body, is also a "vessel." The *OED* defines a lamp not only as a source of illumination, an image which in many ways contradicts the image of a woman "girt" or contained, but also as "a source or centre of light, spiritual or intellectual" (n. "lamp" def. 1d). So while a woman's body must be "girt," her spirit or mind might be allowed to "burn clearly," and she is able to shine, so to speak, spiritually or intellectually. Of course, the image of burning clearly also suggests a kind of limitation and control: a lamp out of control is dangerous, a lamp in control can be put out at the convenience of the user.

The title page of *Monument* also includes representations from biblical scenes that relate to the previous quotation from Luke 12:35 and the conflict present within the text. Depictions of women's roles in biblical history, these images serve the purpose of reminding the (female) reader of both her imperfections and potential. The page includes an image of Eve literally springing forth from Adam, a representation of the Annunciation, and two separate scenes from the parable of the Foolish Virgins. These images frame the title and epithets on either side. At the bottom is an image of a woman, perhaps Elizabeth, holding a "lamp" and a book, with the words "WATCH" and "PRAIE" bracketing her. Each of the biblical images has underneath it a reference to its location in the Bible. Under Eve is "Genesis 3," the chapter in which Eve eats from the apple and Adam and Eve are expelled from the Garden. Under the image of the Annunciation is written "Luke I," which contains the stories of Elizabeth's conception of John the Baptist, as well as the Annunciation. Under the images of the scenes from the parable of the Foolish Virgins is written "Matthew 25," which contains, not surprisingly, the parable of the Wise and Foolish Virgins.

These images also relate to the purpose of the text. For example, the image of Eve bursting forth from Adam's bosom is a figuration of much of the text's own creation. That is to say, the book comes from, and is in some ways part and parcel of, a man—namely, Thomas Bentley. Yet the focus on Eve flying actively away from the languishing Adam suggests a female agency; women are the content and subject of *Monument*. While the text is intended to guide and educate women in proper behavior, the number of works written and translated by women in this text indicates an underlying discourse that goes beyond (flies away from, if you will) the standard patriarchal discourse of other texts written by men.[16] Further, the story from Genesis 3, of Eve (and Adam!) eating the apple and being expelled from the Garden reminds the female reader of Eve's original sin and the subsequent pain in childbirth, subjects with which the *Monument* is concerned. At the same time, the prayers in this text that are intended for use in the event of childbirth suggest a transcendence from this earthly pain, where childbirth becomes a privilege, rather than the burden as suggested in the chapter in Genesis.

The images and references to Matthew 25, the parable of the Wise and Foolish Virgins, also relate specifically to the purpose of the text. The "maidens" who read this text are comparable to the wise and foolish virgins in the parable and illustrations. The parable uses ten maidens with lamps going to meet the bridegroom as a metaphor for women in mortal life aspiring to meet Christ in the kingdom of heaven. Five of the women are foolish because they have their lamps, but no oil, whereas five of the women are wise because they do have oil for their lamps. The wise women are able to find the bridegroom (Christ) when he comes at midnight because they have oil to burn in their lamps, while those without oil must go seek some and subsequently miss the wedding and are shut out from the marriage feast (heaven). The text suggests that if the women who read this are wise, they will "gird their loins" by restricting their sexual behavior and remaining chaste for Christ, the bridegroom. These women will also have oil, that is, knowledge and wisdom, to burn in their lamps so that they may find Christ and not be left out of the wedding feast. The promise of Christ as a bridegroom and reward for wise virginity is held out as a metaphor for the ideal of "married chastity" of Reformation England.

Finally, the quotation from 2 Timothy 19 closes the text on the title page: "Let everie one that calleth upon the name of the Lord depart from iniquitie." This quotation hinges specifically on the idea of free will; it also closes the parable. Paul suggests to Timothy that when he encounters false teachers with "godless chatter," gossip, he must maintain his firm commitment to the Lord: "Avoid...godless chatter, for it will lead people into more and more ungodliness, and their talk will eat its way like gangrene"(2 Timothy 16–18). This passage suggests to the female reader that, in addition to the restrictions and freedoms allowed to her loins (the generative seat), there are also freedoms and restrictions involving the mouth. She can "name the Lord" and be free from iniquity (but restricted in her voice), or she can engage in unbounded "godless chatter" and become depraved and ungodly, and entirely unchaste. This connection of the two orifices—the mouth and the genitals—is a long-standing topos, as is the "problem" women have of keeping both of these orifices shut.[17] The apparent difficulty women have in controlling these orifices is a significant part of what motivates a culture's production of texts like *Monument*.

In keeping with the theme of creating wise and watchful virgins ("undefiled soules"), Bentley fashions in the opening pages a "praier upon the posie prefixed." He writes that as Christians we will "be received to himself [Christ] as those that are made worthie onelie by him, joifullie to enter with him and all the elect and choise wise virgins, into the celestiall wedding chamber of thine eternall kingdome."[18] This further underscores the importance of appropriate behavior and its connection to being received by Christ, the bridegroom. In the celestial wedding chamber, Bentley imagines hand picked and joyful virgins, a community of perfectly chaste and well-behaved women. The "celestial wedding chamber" is heaven, but it is also a wedding chamber, a bedroom, and a place of consummation. Christ is not only the heavenly (and pure and chaste) bridegroom, but he is also the lover.[19] Through this location, Bentley can translate potential sexual and reproductive desires, pleasures, and liberties of speech into a contained, devout, and non-threatening location found in the "celestial" wedding chamber, where spiritual or heavenly consummation and pleasure take the place of physical and material pleasure; prayer takes the place of "godless chatter."

But this binary of closed, quiet, and devout orifices and open, chattering, and profane orifices gets deconstructed in the course of Bentley's Epistle and "Letter to the Good Christian Reader," and in particular through the childbirth prayers in Lamp Five. Bodily and material, and therefore profane, images of pregnancy, childbirth and labor are embedded into discussions of the literary production of "chaste" and godly works. Further, when labor and childbirth are explicitly addressed, as in the case of the childbirth prayers in Lamp five, the religious and spiritual discourse of devotion gets coupled with the physical, emotional, and material discourse of childbirth. These metaphors are a signal of the reproductive unconscious, where the language of the exclusively female experience of birth gets appropriated by men to describe (among other things) the male production of language, particularly through the written word and text. These representations and gaps reveal the culture's anxiety over the female body and its attempt to control and reorganize it.

In Bentley's "Prayer," for example, there are moments when we can see the reproductive unconscious operating. In particular, Bentley links the idea of birth with that of devotional production, such as the production of devotional texts or devotional communities. In the process, he suggests how women's reproductive bodies can or should be used for the increase of piety along with bodily reproduction, but without sexual pleasure. Bentley writes that "we may live soberly to ourselves, Hollie to thee, and uprightly to the world, and thereby gain much profit and fruit to better increase of thy kingdoms."[20] Sober and chaste bodies of women give way to the bodiless "increase" of wisdom, this "increase" echoes the image of God's words to Adam and Eve in Genesis 1.28 to "increase" or reproduce.[21]

Bentley also uses images of labor to describe the process of attaining salvation, using the image of an architectural structure to stand for the body:

> Finallie, make us verie carefullie to keepe this castle of our soules and temple of the holie Ghost (our bodies I mean) pure, holie, and undiefiled... which before all worlds thou hast prepared for thy children, and to receive (of his gift) that which here with deepe sighes and groanes we greatlie long for.[22]

Although a convention, by suggesting the body is a temple and the soul a castle Bentley reveals a discomfort with and attraction to the vulnerability and fallibility of the body, especially the female body.[23] That is to say, by concretizing and representing the body as a "temple" or "castle," Bentley makes it less vulnerable than the mortal flesh. Further, by endowing the architectural "body" with spiritual and noble markers (like a temple and castle), he reminds the reader of the goal of a true Christian and English subject. Yet these structures of soul and body alike are the intended receptacles prepared for "thy children." And, like a woman in labor who greatly longs for delivery, "we" as Christians sigh and groan in longing for "our" delivery to God.

In his Epistle, Bentley links the idea of literary production with childbirth and the laboring body with the divine, further suggesting the reproductive unconscious and the power of the reproductive image. The Epistle opens with Bentley situating God as a great lover and believer of England through his placement of Elizabeth on the throne, and by recounting how Elizabeth was appointed to govern the realm of England by God Himself. Bentley then envisions England as a kind of Eden where every "man sitting under his vine and fig tree throughout all your dominions, dooth give...occasion to the godlie to be no lesse thankfull to God, and your Maiestie."[24] Bentley sets up the image of a fertile and masculine location of Eden with men sitting under fig trees throughout Elizabeth's realm. One could argue that the image of being thankful to Elizabeth (as well as to God) suggests that Elizabeth had a role in the production and creation of the nation (and the men who inhabit it). And, while Elizabeth is a woman, she is a notoriously virginal figure, even at times masculinized, and often problematic.[25] Bentley in his Edenic England describes his masculine role in producing the text in terms of female images. He wants

> to offer something. Wherein I might bring profit to that mysticall bodie, wherof I trust I am a member. And persuading myself, I could not better employ my labour to the good of the church. And now in most dutifull manner commending and appropriating so divine exercises of the church, unto your majestie the most naturall mother and noble nursse therof; the cause of a virgin to a Virgine, the works of Queenes to a Queene; to accept these your leige subject his great labors and painfull travels[26] in good part.[27]

The maternal—mother, nurse, caregiver—gets collapsed here at times with the masculine. Bentley, in bringing "profit" to the "mystical" body of the church, which is commonly considered female, blurs the distinction between the masculine production of a text and the physical labor of birth. In addressing Queen Elizabeth as the "most natural mother and noble nurse," to whom he presents "the cause of a virgin to a Virgin," Bentley imagines Elizabeth as the Virgin Mother (Mary) one of the figures after whom she so diligently fashioned herself. While the image of Mary invokes the image of a virgin and painless birth, Bentley represents himself as suffering the painful travails of labor in producing the work for Elizabeth. His collapsing in this metaphor of the masculine production of language (text) with the labor of childbirth parallels his collapsing of Elizabeth as the material natural mother and the mystical virgin. It also is a perfect example of Bentley's complicated relationship to the female reproductive body.

Further, in his letter "To the Christian Reader, grace and truth in Christ," Bentley imagines the women who produced the texts as extraordinarily intelligent and industrious, and he is particularly interested in their relationship to devotional, goodly and "godlie" works. In his more than seven-page epistle, Bentley describes women such as Elizabeth I, Katherine Parr, and other "godlie Gentlewomen of al ages," as having "given" their bodies to their writings. In so doing, these women essentially leave behind the female material production of flesh for the more masculine and chaste production of texts or "godlie works." He imagines them as "even from their tender & maidenlie yeares to spend their time, their wits, their substance, and also their bodies, in the studies of noble and approved sciences."[28] In order for a woman to produce a goodly work, she must literally empty or spend her "substance" and body. Nowhere, however, does he use this metaphor to describe how these women labored to create their texts as he himself has done to create this one.

Also in his letter, Bentley imagines what the female textual community looks like who might take up and read this text. He describes his work as compiled in such a way as to have "plaine, easie, familiar, and certeine method order, and direction, both for matter and maner, as I could possiblie devise, or was requisite for such a worke, to make it profitable to the simple and unlearned reader."[29] While Bentley describes works such as Margareite de Navarre's as "above all, the most divine, learned, and godlie treatise," he sees the audience for this text as simple and unlearned, and only able to latch on to that which is "familiar." Bentley also imagines that the women who would read these texts should do so in private: "more proper and peculiar for the private use of women, that heretofore hath beene set out by anie."[30] By designing a text which is to be read most properly in private, Bentley assures himself and the culture that these women will be separate and remain chaste, rather than get together for "godless chatter," and therefore potentially adulterous activity.

While assuring good literacy behaviors of the readers he imagines above, Bentley also gives a model of the "maternal" relationship of reader to text. At the end of his letter and the description of the text, Bentley proposes that the relationship between the female authors and the readers is similar to that between a mother and her daughter (which parallels to some degree that between the church—female, mother—and followers):

> I might hereby, as much as in me lieth, incourage, provoke, and allure all godlie women of our time, in some measure, according to their severall gifts given them of God, to become even from their youth more studious imitators, and diligent followers of so godlie and rare examples in their vertuous mothers they may shine also together with them on earth, as burning lampes of verie virginity.[31]

Bentley describes the formation of a particular female textual community; he will "allure" young maidens to be imitators of their textual "mothers." He will cajole even the youngest (or perhaps particularly the youngest) to become diligent followers and "shine altogether" with their virtuous mothers. He must "provoke" and "incourage" these women with all that "lieth" within him.

In the course of this description, Bentley seems to take pleasure in emptying himself out, as the women who produced the texts contained in his compilation did, in order to bring all these chaste women together. On the other hand, the virtuous mothers and young women, "studious imitators," also represent, like Queen Elizabeth herself, a kind of bodiless, sexless virgin. Bentley also comes full circle by ending this section with the image from the title page. He invokes the image of the wise and foolish virgins with their lamps through the phrase "burning lampes of verie virginity." At this point in the text, the reader has the choice of either following the "maternal" text and burning their wise, virginal lamps, or of being foolish, lightless, and motherless.

CHILDBIRTH PRAYERS IN *THE MONUMENT OF MATRONES*: DEVOTION AND BIRTH RITUAL MEET

The childbirth prayers in *Monument* show the complexity of the early modern maternal experience, setting up certain traditional models of patriarchal expectations of appropriate maternal behavior while at the same time suggesting that the woman's role in childbirth is a privileged one, particularly in relationship to God and Christ. The text expresses these conflicting roles on the one hand through its male-authorized traditional discourses that require and desire chaste and contained women. On the other hand, it expresses these conflicting roles through the ways in which the ritual of birth is figured as a location where female power and knowledge—of midwives, mothers and attendants—becomes sanctified. The relationship of the prayers in Lamp Five with the female body is, for the most part, a harmonious one, if sometimes distant in physiological terms. But occasionally the author reveals a distinct discomfort with the female body; at one point the speaker refers to herself as "thy most difiled and polluted hand-maid," full of "unworthiness, vilenes, and uncleannes."[32] The prayers for midwives present for the most part a person of gentle, dedicated, and diligent character, a portrayal which is in conflict with many representations of midwives in male-authored midwifery manuals such as the popular *The Byrth of Mankynde*. The childbirth prayers and the framework of the Fifth Lamp show the complex expectations and roles of the mother, gossip, and attendant in the childbirth scene and cultural attitudes toward fertility and childbirth.

BENTLEY IMPLIES HIS READERS

The layout and content of opening pages of *Monument* imply a particular use for the text. As mentioned above, there is evidence that parts of *Monument* could have been published as individual pamphlets, given the nature of the discrete title pages for some of the lamps, including Lamp Five. Lamp Five has its own set of page numbers, 1–212, and is followed by a table of contents.[33] The "table of contents" style listing of prayers and meditations suggests that women would desire or need to look up a particular prayer for a particular occasion. Lamp Four also contains a concluding list of "principall praiers and meditation," prayers intended for use on particular holy days, hours, times, and seasons of the year "both at home, and also in the Church, at convenient times permitted."[34] Both lamps include prayers for specific occasions, which apparently warrant a list. The kinds of prayers in Lamp Four have a precedent in medieval *Book of Hours* and any number of early modern devotional manuals. If Lamp Five was published as a separate pamphlet, as its composition suggests, its size and content would make it quite suitable for private use in a house, chamber, or birthing area by one or several women.

The "title" page of Lamp Five contains a description of the purpose of the prayers and meditations contained within, as well as the intended audience:

> The Fift Lampe of Virginitie: Conteining sundrie forms of christian praiers and meditations, to be used onlie of and for all sorts and degrees of women, in their severall ages and callings; as namelie, of virgins, wives, women with child, Midwives, Mothers, Daughters, Mistresses, Maids, Widowes, and old women. A treatise verie needfull for this time, and profitable to the Church: now newlie compiled to the glorie of God, & comfort of al godlie women, by the said T.B. Gentleman.[35]

In "To the Christian Reader," Bentley suggests that his text is appropriate for an educationally diverse range of potential readers, including Queen Elizabeth, and that his text is "profitable to the simple and unlearned reader."[36] Like "To the Christian Reader," the opening of Lamp Five shows Bentley imagining an audience that includes "all sorts and degrees" of women, including rich and poor, young and old, wives and widows, mistresses and maids, mothers and daughters; this includes, we assume, learned and unlearned women. It is also important to Bentley that the reader—or perhaps the reader's husband, father, brother, or priest—understand how "profitable" this text is for the Church, that his text promises to make new and better Christian and chaste women.[37] Further, there is some indication that the culture lacks texts "profitable" for women, and this one presumably answers that need by supplying works (some of which have been previously published) that address and express the experience of women. This work, then, exhibits and answers both the needs of the "dominant" culture, and the traditionally subordinate female "subculture." *Monument* promises to aid in the "proper" and approved development of all types of women, while also speaking to a "female," and a potentially dissident, gossiping, community.

The illustration that borders the title page of Lamp Five shows representations of Queen Elizabeth, Abishag, Martha, and Sarepta, kneeling in prayer (Figure 3). By representing these women and men in a subordinate position, the text fulfills its patriarchal obligation. But it also, in the act of representing these women at all, creates a space for, or at least an identifiable location for, women to practice their devotions. In addition to a skull in the bottom part of the border as a reminder of our mortality (and following the printer information and date of publication), there is a quotation from Matthew 26:46: "Watch and praie, that ye enter not into temptation: the spirit is readie, but the flesh is weake,"[38] reminding the female reader of her potential toward corrupt flesh. The Biblical quotation is

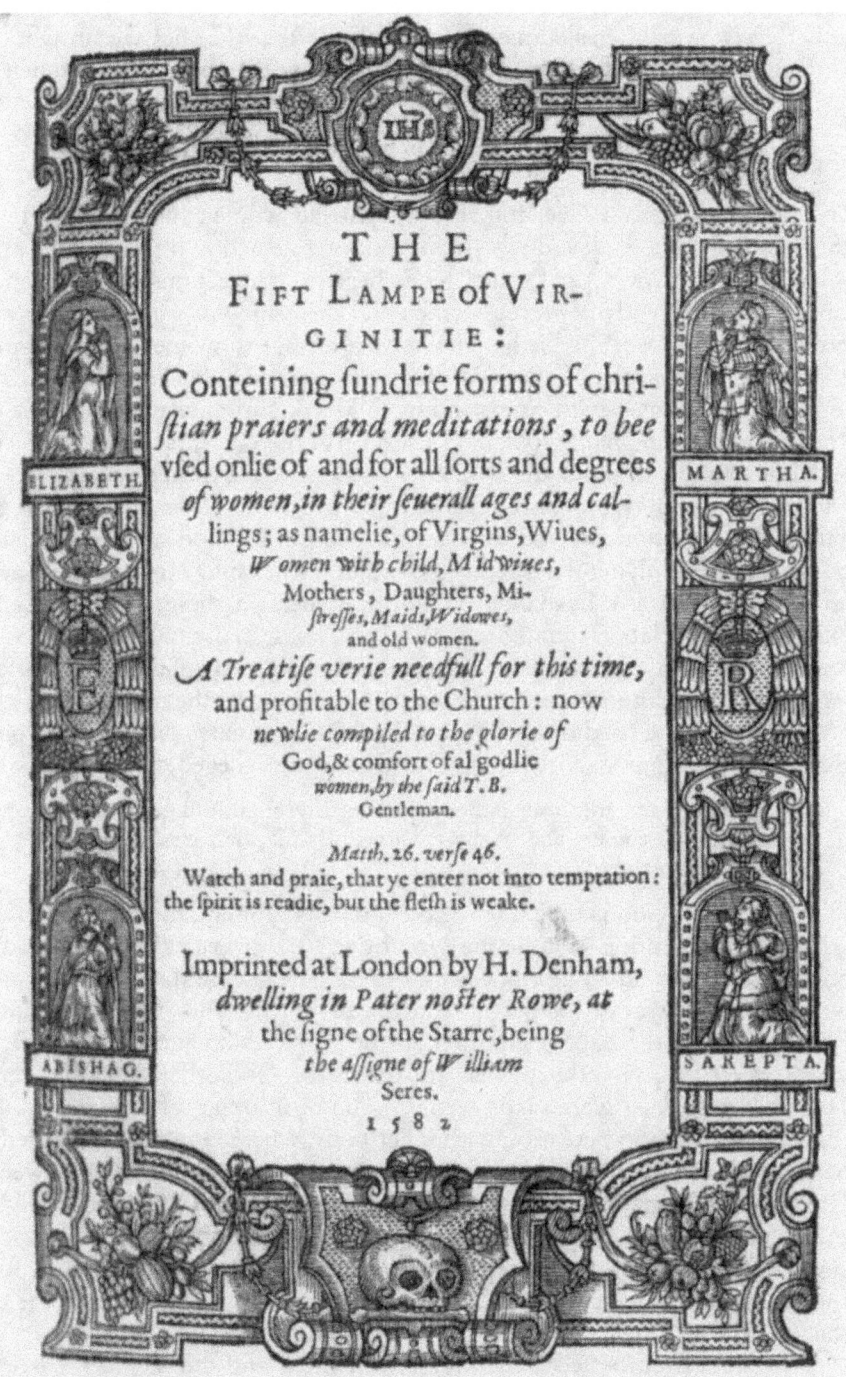

Figure 3. Front page of Lamp Five of Thomas Bentley's *Monument of Matrones* (1582). This item is reproduced by permission of *The Huntington Library, San Marino, California.*

rather conventional and commonplace, but the text that lies within works against it in several ways, mainly by articulating the strength of women's devotional prowess in the face of intense physical pain and anxiety.

"GREEFE UNSPEAKABLE": THE BODY IN LABOR PAIN

The prayers in Lamp Five, for virgins, married women (before and after childbearing age), and widows, number more than one hundred and are valuable in their own right, but I focus here on the sections for pregnant, laboring, and recently delivered women and their midwives because of their explicit depictions of the birth scene in relationship to women's association with God. This section of about 38 prayers is marked by the header "Praiers to be said of women with child, and in childbed, and after their deliverie." The prayers for pregnant women, like several of the later prayers for women in labor, show the pregnant woman as having a privileged, even sacred relationship to God and Christ through her pregnancy. Some present pregnancy as a creation of God and use the notion of God as the ultimate creator, while implying that God is the father of the child—in fact, there are no references to any husbands or mortal fathers in these prayers at all. Others align the laboring mother with Mary. Thus, many of the prayers for pregnant women express through spiritual terms very explicit physical elements of childbirth in order to negotiate the virgin and the mother.

"A praier to be used of a woman with child" intimates that the relationship between the pregnant woman and God is a privileged one. It begins:

> O Almightie and mercifull father, which of thy bountifull goodnes hast fructified my wombe, and of thy gracious blessing, hast created in me a reasonable creature.[39]

In this passage, God is the father of the laboring woman, the husband, and creator. In presenting God as the "fructifier," the prayer alludes to God's relationship to women in biblical narratives, suggesting that the pregnant woman is like Sarah, Rebekah, and Leah in the Old Testament, and Elizabeth, John the Baptist's mother, in the New Testament. These women were barren, but by the power and grace of God, their wombs were "opened" and they were made fertile.[40] The positioning of the woman as the recipient of God's creation within her body, where God has "fructified" her womb, also implies a sanctified and transcendent relationship between God and the woman. The woman is like Mary in that the "gracious blessing" of the fructified womb suggests a kind of virginal conception. By using such terms as "bountiful" and "fructified" to describe the pregnant state, the woman in labor combines images of virginal conception with that of the sumptuous and bountiful Garden of Eden.

The connection between the pregnant woman and the sacred is carried on in the woman's acceptance of women's "lot" in childbirth, and in her request for an uneventful and safe pregnancy and delivery:

> I acknowledge, O Lord, that justlie for our sinfull transgression of thy commandments, thou saiedst unto the first woman, our grand mother Eve, and in hir to us all; I will increse thy sorowe, when thou are with child: with paine shalt thou bring foorth thy children.[41]

As she anticipates her labor, the woman acknowledges that womankind's transgressions are "justly" punished by God, and she embraces her own sinful nature by situating herself with "our grand mother Eve, and in hir to us all." Further, in this prayer, God is represented as making this woman (and perhaps all women) pregnant, an image that elevates women to the position of a "wife" to God, that is, like the Virgin Mary. While Mary is present implicitly, the woman's body is not mediated through Mary's experience explicitly as in this text's pre-Reformation counterparts, and the woman's primary relationship is to Christ and God, rather than to Mary. Thus, the Biblical notion of connecting pain to childbirth is predictably iterated and seemingly accepted.

But while the patriarchal voice might be satisfied in this admission of original sin, the author also seems to turn this notion upside down. Instead of women being placed under the relentless burden of their sinful flesh, as evidenced by her pregnant and sinful body, the lines immediately following this section set up the act of labor in terms of a sacrifice:

> All our paines therefore that we suffer in this behalfe, are none other thing, but a worthie cross laid upon us by the godlie ordinance, to the which with hart & mind I humblie submit my selfe, trusting surelie, and being fullie persuaded in my faith, that thou callest none into perill and danger, but both thou canst, and wilt at convenient season deliver them.[42]

The pains of labor are, like Christ's sufferings, not a punishment of the woman's own sin but rather a "worthie cross laid upon us by the godlie ordinance." The image of the worthy cross laid on the back of the pregnant woman suggests a sacred duty of sacrifice, one that is not the result of sexual desire or lustful folly, but rather comes out of divine "ordinance." Like Christ, she submits herself to the pain of the birth as he does to the cross, believing that, in the end, she will be "delivered," both from her sins, and from her infant. Placing the pain in childbirth in the context of Christ's crucifixion elevates the mortal and sinful bodily experience to a sacred, transcendent experience, and one in which the pregnant woman is persuaded she will be delivered both spiritually and physically.

Of course, the image of delivery here is multi-fold. Conflating delivery of a child with delivery from sins with Christ's delivery and deliverance of us from our sins creates a poignant friction within the text. One kind of delivery is based on the purity of the soul, the other kind of delivery is predicated on the sins of the flesh. This coupling of delivery from sins and delivery of a child is commonplace throughout the childbirth prayers. It functions to suggest the way in which the binary of the sacred soul and sinful flesh is reconfigured in the course of this text, so that it is the very flesh that empowers women to speak virtuously and powerfully. It also becomes the occasion for men to infiltrate the female voice and birth scene by making the prayers available and by framing their presentation.[43]

While it is easy to imagine a pregnant woman uttering the prayers intended for her, one essential dilemma raised by the prayers intended to be said by women while in labor lies in imagining how these prayers might be practiced. Elaine Scarry's basic premise about pain is that "physical pain does not simply resist language but actively destroys it."[44] And while Scarry doesn't speak to labor pain specifically, her formulation about pain in general, and particularly pain through torture, is useful in discussing pain in childbirth. I would argue that the physiology of childbirth makes it difficult, if not impossible, to speak during the contractions of labor; speech during contractions is neither rational nor coherent, but rather comes from "a state anterior to language."[45] The question, then, arises: how is it that women are supposed to utter sometimes pages of prayer while in labor? The answers to this question are of course as complicated as they are varied, but they are potentially useful in understanding several main issues involved in moving childbirth from an unconscious to a conscious part of the culture. On the one hand, childbirth is indescribable because the intense experience of the pain of labor precludes a language to define it. Without a language or "text" to define the experience of childbirth, it exists outside the symbolic order, and therefore in a sense cannot be articulated textually. On the other hand, it is perhaps through the pain of labor that these women, in some sense, are "made" and become empowered to speak, as suggested by the previous prayer which figures labor as a holy sacrifice, rather than a justifiable punishment.

Through the problem of pain in labor, the representation of childbirth in these prayers suggests the ways in which the culture imagines the ritual and the ways in which the culture desires to manage or define that ritual. At times it is as if Bentley as publisher provides these words, supplying the voice for the laboring, voiceless woman, while the woman supplies the body. Elaine Scarry also argues that "the place of man and the place of God in the human generation that so dominates Genesis are easy to separate from one another: the place of man is in the body; the place of God is in the voice. The narrative records momentous alteration in the human body."[46] In this case, Bentley acts here in the place of God who "houses" or is mediator to the voice of the laboring female, while the woman occupies the place of the body.

On the other hand, the inability of a laboring woman actually to speak these prayers on her own does not discount their value in the situation of birth, for they might be uttered to herself in a meditational manner, or by a midwife or other female attendant, friend, or relative. The latter is the most likely possibility, since pain in childbirth also precludes, by corollary, rational thought, and because during pauses or rests between contractions women naturally tend to conserve energy. The heading to one of the prayers for women in labor suggests both the possibility that the pregnant woman or an attendant might utter the prayer: "The praier in long and dangerous trauell of child, to be vsed either of the woman hirself, or by the women about hir in hir behalfe."⁴⁷ In this same prayer, the speaker actually expresses to God that the pain of the contractions she is experiencing in childbirth are "intollerable, and the greefe unspeakeable."⁴⁸ Scenarios like these, in which the speaker's voice could be seen either as a male "imitation" of a female experience or an "actual" female voice, give us a sense of the infiltration of a male voice into a female ritual, as well as a glimpse into the ritual of childbirth, however altered these prayers might be by a potentially male author or male editor.

Several of the prayers specifically intended for women in labor and the one for women who are having a particularly difficult labor often conflate physical labor in childbirth with spiritual labor. This conflation makes available to us certain social expectations of childbirth, of the "actual" or perceived physical space and experience of childbirth, of the community that enables the ritual, and of the cultural attitudes toward the social scene. These prayers of conflict and conflation suggest a relationship between textual, birth, and devotional communities. One such prayer is the aforementioned "The praier in long and dangerous travell of child, to be used either of the woman in hir selfe, or by the women about hir in hir behalfe." Like many of the childbirth prayers, including the one quoted above, this prayer exhibits some of the standard language of sin and forgiveness. But it also stands out as a prayer that seems to paint a more elaborate and even intimate picture of the childbirth process. The title suggests that there is recognition that the woman may be incapable of uttering the prayer herself, and so the "women about hir in hir behalfe" might read the prayer. The idea that the prayer could be read by women attending a woman in labor implies that Bentley, and presumably the culture at large, had a sense of a female birth community where at least one, and presumably more, of the women were literate. This also suggests, as this Lamp in general does, a necessary relationship between female textual and birth communities.

While almost all of the prayers dedicated to women in labor mention at least one occasion the "greivous groanes," "deepe sighes," "pinching panges," or "deepe greefes" that are a result of labor, this prayer is unique in that it pays attention to some of the physiological elements of birth in ways that most of the other prayers do not. It refers to explicit physiologic events particular to the process of childbirth and beyond the acknowledgement of pain in labor. For example, the prayer describes what appears to be a breathing technique of the woman in labor:

> For lo, thou seest, how I pant with paine, and grone through griefe, and travell in sore labour before thee, togither with all thy creatures, sighing

in my selfe, and waiting for thy readie helpe, and my speedie deliverance foorth of this distres.[49]

This is essentially a description of how a woman might respond to labor pains, by panting and groaning through the contractions, where "griefe" in fact is not only "hardship, suffering," but is also "physical pain or discomfort" (*OED*, n. "grief" def.3). This description also suggests that the experience of pain in labor is a very personal and private one, where the woman is "sighing in my selfe." The "sighing in my selfe" also suggests a private meditation with God, which is the way this prayer is meant to function. While the woman acknowledges her pain outwardly with groans and pants, and while the experience of pain is also a very personal one, the text suggests that this is also a group event. God sees the woman in "sore labour" (is there any other kind?) "togither with all thy creatures," where "all thy creatures" suggests her several female attendants. This description has a spiritual connotation in that the women are situated as "creatures" of God. But the duty of the midwife, and perhaps even the work of the laboring mother, becomes elided as she waits for God to deliver her speedily from her distress.

Later on, the prayer also describes other even less glamorous and more explicitly physiological elements of the childbirth process in spiritual terms. These descriptions come in a lament that echoes the sentiments of several other of the prayers, but in addition to the common pleas for "speedie deliverance" and a rescue of the "languishing soule," the prayer goes on to ask for relief from very specific ailments:

> How long shall my bowels thus sound like an harpe, my bones and sinewes be racked asunder, and my inward parts be thus greevouslie tormented for my sins? Consider, O Lord, how I am troubled, how my wombe is disquieted, and my hart wambleth within me for anguish.[50]

The "bowels [that] thus sound like an harpe" refer to the flatulence that sometimes accompanies the process of the child moving down the birth canal. The "bones and sinewes be racked asunder" refers to the loosening of tendons and ligaments as a result of hormones released in late pregnancy. The prayer also makes more metaphoric and spiritual allusions to the birth process in describing the contracting uterus as a "disquieted" womb, an image that parallels the state of the woman's spirit. By using the word "wambleth" to describe the sensation of a distressed heart, the prayer continues to conflate the experience of spiritual distress, as suffered in this case metaphorically in the heart, with distress in childbirth. "Wambleth" is a form of "wamble," which commonly refers to the sensation of "the stomach or its contents: to be felt to roll about (in nausea)" (*OED*, "wamble" def.1b), or "to turn and twist the body about, roll or wriggle about, roll over and over" (*OED*, "wamble" def. 2). In childbirth, a woman often experiences a sensation of nausea in the final stages of birth. "Wambleth," then, could refer to the turning and twisting infant inside the mother's womb. Further, the experience of intense pain in birth might cause a woman to turn and twist her own body, or to roll about in anguish or in hopes of discovering a more comfortable position, just as woman (or man) might writhe in anguish in a state of spiritual torment.[51] This experience is transferred in the prayer to a spiritual level in which the heart or soul feels a type of "disquiet" at the unknown spiritual and physical outcome. This collapse of the sanctioned spiritual reverie and the intense, physical, private birth experience figures childbirth as an anguish that only God can relieve, reducing feminine agency in both quarters.

The text embodies the subjection and abjection of women through meanings attached to childbirth, expressing themselves through the "oppressed" physical condition of labor, highlighting the nature of women's social as well as physical oppression, and in so doing finding a voice for that same oppression:

> Oh Lord, am not I a wofull wight, who with all the sorrowes of a travelling woman, am oppressed in thy sight. Yea, thou seest in what pitifull plight I am, drawing nigh towards my travell, and hearest me sorrowfull wretch crieng out in my pangs, as she that is destitute of all mortall helpe.[52]

This passage suggests that it is the "sorrows of a travailing woman" that not only make her a woeful spirit, but that oppress her in the sight of God. By the context we understand her to be in labor, and yet the syntax also suggests that God sees her as a "woeful spirit" who, like the laboring woman, is full of similar sorrows and is oppressed by them. It is through these sorrows that God sees what a "pitiful" situation she is in, and cannot help but hear the "crying out in her pangs," especially as she has been brought to the end of her tether, fearing she will die, as expressed by the phrase "destitute of all mortall helpe."

The text of the prayer also demonstrates women's particular conundrum relative to filling the desires of the culture by being obedient and silent in the face of extreme anxiety and pain. And, in contrast to the groaning and crying out in birth, the prayer expresses, rather unusually I think, the woman's unique relationship to God through both silence and sobbing:

> I have a long time, O Lord, held my peace, suppressing my throwes so long as my womanlie strength will suffer. I have beene quiet and still, and restrained my selfe, I saie, as much as I am able.[53]

The prayer expresses how a woman might feel trying to abide by the doctrine of silence as an attribute of Godly behavior, plaintively uttering to God that she has "held her peace" for as long as she has been able to. In addition to speech, the woman also feels compelled to "suppress" her pain as long as her "womanlie strength will suffer." It takes a great deal of control to remain "quiet and still" during active labor; in fact, at some point it is quite impossible. Finally, the woman is in such intense physical and emotional pain that she must give in to her need to cry and groan:

> ...but now alas, such and so intollerable is my græfe, so manie and vehement are my throwes, yea, so continuall and tedious is my travell, that without thee, I can not possiblie anie longer forbeare, but am forced through bodilie paine, and inward greefe, to shrich and crie alowd unto thee, and that with teares, for speedie comfort and heavenlie helpe, that the which is in sore labour, may find mitigation of hir paines, through thy mercie, and being readie to bring foorth, may be delivered through thy power.[54]

The physical pain of birth is described here as "continual and tedious," which is a rather odd way to describe an experience that appears from the description to be intense physically and emotionally. "Tedious" is a term which suggests something is "wearisome.long and tiresome" (OED, n. "tedious" def. 1) and might better describe an occurrence that is boring, rather than one which usually is accompanied by emotional distress and physical anguish. Further, the expression of pain in this manner is a means of gaining God's attention.

In this passage, as in others discussed above, the image of physical childbirth is brought together with the spiritual. A point of conflation occurs at the moment when the woman describes what drives her, finally, from her forbearance of utterance to shrieks and cries. This occurs at the time when the woman is so overwhelmed by both her bodily pain and her inward grief that she is forced to break her sacred silence, and this cry brings her closer to God. The woman's voice is most heard when she is least capable of speaking. For the woman it is through her female experience of birth, which is the manifestation of sinful, "weak," and female flesh, that a woman can make a sacred space in order to express a singularly female and particular relationship to God. Many places in this prayer, as in other prayers noted above, it is God who gives, or rather has the potential to give, "heavenly help" from sore labor and mitigation from pains, as in the case of the Virgin birth. It is also God who has the power, so it seems to the laboring woman, to both "shut up the doors of her wombe" and halt the progress of labor and also to "make a way out for my deliverance."[55]

The prayer suggests that it is in part because of God's role in the production of the child that he will be the agent of its delivery:

> It is thou onlie, O Lord my God, which hast fashioned it in my wombe, that must doo it. Oh therefore put forth speedile thine almightie hand, and helpe me.[56]

Again, the relationship of God to the laboring woman is implicitly like that of God to the Virgin Mary in that it is God "only," not a man, who has "fashioned" or impregnated the woman. But also in putting forth his hands (and hopefully speedily), it is God who is requested to act as a midwife, and in this request the prayer elides the actual midwife. In fact, God is described as the agent of the laboring woman's own birth when she, in arguing for a speedy and safe delivery, states "Oh Lord, thou art he that hast drawne me out of my mothers womb long since."[57] In bringing God into this female realm, this substitution serves to bring out the Godliness of midwives, while undermining their medical efficacy.

The description given of how the laboring mother imagines God's assistance is reminiscent of the enclosed scene of a birth ritual, as well as a place for private (textual) devotion. She summons not only God, but also the "holie Ghost," and she imagines the Trinity coming into her spiritual and birth space:

> O blessed trinitie, come visit a wretch that now (as thou seest) is entred into hir secret chamber, and hath shut the dores about hir to hide hir selfe for a little while, untill thine indignation be overpassed.[58]

The laboring woman invites the Holy Trinity (Father, Son and Holy Ghost) to her "secret chamber" where she then shuts the doors and hides for a little while. The secret place that the woman enters represents a place of private devotion, which is reminiscent of the enclosures of monks and mystics (and the textual and studious nature of their enclosures). It also is suggestive of the way the Protestant movement encouraged private devotion, which seems to have been particularly appealing to women. The secret chamber that the laboring woman has entered is also evocative of the ritualistically enclosed birthing space in which all doors and windows are sealed and covered to keep out all light and all men (see Chapter One). Also, the male desire to infiltrate this space comes through the woman's prayer and can be seen in the fact that the laboring woman requests that the three of the Trinity accompany her in this sanctified space of the female birthing enclosure. Yet these men are not really "men" in the sense that God and Christ are in some way seen as compassionate, forgiving, and even maternal figures, as illustrated in Julian of Norwich's *Book of Shewings* and her *Revelations of Divine Love*.[59] Given this vision, the woman then constructs for herself a truly sanctified enclosure, with God as midwife, and the Son and Holy Ghost as her attendants or "gossips."

The prayer, in suggesting God be the personal attendant to the laboring woman, excludes the female community in which women have an opportunity to support and express themselves. The woman's prayer implies a negotiation; to gain a painless and speedy delivery at the hand of God, the woman subtly, rhetorically, gives up her female gossips and midwife and to some degree allows the text to become a replacement for the female community. Yet by imagining this community of holy attendants, which in a sense feminizes them, the prayer undermines those same communities that it recognizes. The act of being called upon to deliver the woman's child, then, marks both a recognition and foreclosing of the kind of female birth community that the text sets up as integral to the female birth ritual.

This prayer also reveals the complexity of the reproductive unconscious in that the passage brings together the suspicion of what occurs between women in the birth chamber with the desire to gain access to that chamber, while presenting the participants as sacred (the Holy Trinity) but also female (birth attendants). In the previous excerpt, the laboring woman invites the Trinity to come visit her in her "secret chamber." She now requests God to "work his works" in secret: "Come, I saie, O glorious and almightie God, come speedilie, and through thy divine power worke thou all our workes for us heere in secret, that we may praise thee openlie."[60] This passage resonates with the idea of a sanctified "gossiping" in which "secrets" are told and knowledge is disseminated. The pronoun shifts to the first person plural when the laboring woman asks that God "through divine power work thou all our works for *us* here in secret" (my emphasis). The prayer here imagines the birth ritual as similar to the praying in secret suggested in Matthew 6.6: "When you pray go into your room and shut the door and pray to your Father who is in secret; and your Father who sees in secret will reward you." But while this passage brings to mind this famous biblical passage, it also suggests that the work is the work of female birth attendants, not of God or men. If God represents the patriarchal mechanism by which women's behavior is managed, God's role as divine interventionist indicates a desire to enter into the one location where men have historically had little influence: in the "secret" childbirth chamber. This birth space, as we have seen above, can also be read as a divine enclosure sanctified by God's presence as the midwife, but to the exclusion of mortal men.

The passage in this prayer particularly echoes the "privy" knowledge that *Trotula* insists upon preserving and that *The Byrth of Mankynd* insists that it reveals. Similar then to both *Byrth* and *Trotula*, the text of the childbirth prayers, among others in *Monument*, plays a part in the economy of the dissemination of knowledge. That is, through the publication of a text explicitly intended for women which addresses specifically female experiences, the text seeks to reveal, and to some degree control, that which is secret—the ritual of birth. By revealing and in a sense publicizing that which is normally secret, *Monument* in some way removes the power of the secretive ritual, at the same time the text also, through more subtle means, re-inscribes and reveals the value of these secret and private devotional and birth practices.

"OF THIS MY CALLING": PRAYERS FOR MIDWIVES

Lamp Five contains three prayers explicitly intended for use and utterance by midwives, all of which follow the prayers intended for laboring Queens and prayers for women "in general": "A praier to be said of everie Christian midwife for hir selfe, before she execute hir office," "Another praier to be said of the midwife, when she goeth about to doo hir office," and "In doing hir office, let the midwife praie thus with hir selfe."[61] These prayers for midwives, like many of the other childbirth prayers, reveal the culture's anxiety about midwives and pregnant women, while also setting up the relationship between midwives and God as a special and privileged one. They explicitly address the nature of the office of midwife, hinting at the culture's concern, even distress, over their imagined lack of competency. Such concerns, as I have noted above, are voiced in many popular texts of the day, most notably in the multi-edition *The Byrth of Mankynd*. The image of the incompetent midwife is countered, however, by a representation of the midwife as conscientious and professional, even as Godly. It is difficult, of course, to determine whether this is an expression of a social desire for midwives to behave in a Godly fashion, and therefore the subsequent promise through these texts that they will be less threatening, or whether this is an expression of the female midwife's expertise, ability, and Godliness. The prayers also imagine female birth, devotional, and textual communities through the representation of those participants in childbirth and through prayers particularly designed to be led by the midwife and uttered by the women attendants.

The first of these three prayers for midwives, like several of the prayers intended for laboring women, points to the historical position of the laboring woman and midwife in particular relation to childbirth and sin. This first prayer situates women's laboring bodies relative to the Fall. The prayer first concentrates on the prelapsarian birth experience in which God

> at the beginning didst appoint woman to be the organe, instrument, and befell to receive, nourish, & bring foorth man through thy wonderfull workmanship without anie labour, paine, or help of flesh and blood.[62]

This return to Eden imagines an unmediated birth in which the child born is the result of God's "workmanship." This image brings to mind not just the image of the Virgin Birth, but also the many prayers in this Lamp that make use of the image of God as the creator of the baby not yet born.

But just as this prayer echoes images of God as the "fructifier" of women's wombs, the opening passage also recounts the "disobedience of our grandmother Eve." Not only is this description a ubiquitous account of woman's role in man's fall and women's subsequent pain in childbirth, it also uses this original "disobedience" as the touchstone for the necessity of the midwife: "that which before was easie, now to become hard and painefull, yea dangerous and impossible." The role of the midwife in the face of "dangerous and impossible" labor is to "help & ease woman, which through their owne imperfection and feebleness are not able in this case and time of their sore labour, to helpe themselves."[63] The phrase "their own imperfection" may suggest that either the midwife is removed or beyond the experience of labor or sin (midwives, in fact, were often older women without young children to tend to and were often widows). It may also suggest there is some slippage in the "voice" of the prayer, revealing an accusatory patriarchal voice. Still, the prayer gives an indication of both the subordinate notion of women (as midwives) as well as the necessity of women as birth attendants: "[God] as a meane hast ordeined man to be a god to man, and made woman through thine unspeakable power working togither with him, to helpe & ease woman."[64] God has very specifically and explicitly ordained as a "meane," or mediator, man to govern man, and, working together with him, he has made woman through his "unspeakable power" to help laboring women help themselves.

The midwife, working together with God, is represented within the prayer both as the humble servant and as a divine agent. The midwife is situated as "thy most unworthie hand-maid to the office of a midwife among the daughters of Israel." By locating the midwife in biblical history, the text supports the notion of the Godliness of the office of midwife "among the daughters of Israel." Yet she is also an "unworthy handmaid" in relation to God, and she functions in a traditional role of servitude. But while the "handmaid" is an image of servitude, it can also be an honored and ordained position, as suggested in the following passage:

> ...and [God] made me an instrument and means under thee to comfort them in their sorrowes, cherish them in their child-beds, ease them in their pains, and to further them in their deliverance, with all possible paines and convenient speede that I may, and can, in thee and for thee.[65]

In God "making" the midwife in order to fill a particular and important office, this passage answers the many prayers of women in labor who request from God a less painful labor and a speedy delivery. In taking up these requests made specifically to God, the midwife herself plays a God-ordained role ("in thee and for thee"). So while she answers to and works on behalf of God, she also does so in his place. In this case, the midwife is both a mediator for, and usurper of, God's role in delivering the laboring woman.

In addition to presenting the midwife as Godly, the prayer expresses and delineates some of the contemporary criticisms and fears about midwives through the midwife's request for a release from them:

> Take me from all ignorance, negligence, slouthfulnes, slacknes, and disdaine; yea from all unmercifulnes, rough handling, hardnes of hart, contempt of others, falshood, cruelties, and bloudgiltiness, good Lord deliver me.[66]

The prayer acknowledges some of the major complaints about midwives, many of which are voiced in *The Byrth of Mankynde* and *The Rose Garden for Pregnant Women and Midwives*, particularly the characteristics of ignorance, neglect, and rough handling.[67] At the same time, the prayer counters this anxiety about midwives through a list of very positive and admirable traits the midwife asks for in lieu of the unsavory ones:

> and in steed thereof, make me wise-harted, skilfull, loving, gentle, tender, pitifull cherefull, comfortable, helpfull, painefull, watchfull, strong, able, readie, willing, carefull, diligent, & faithfull, even for thy sake onelie, without respect of filthie lucre, to pleasure all women at all times in my calling, to the full discharge of my conscience and dutie.[68]

The prayer describes a midwife who desires not only skillfulness and readiness in her professional office, but also empathy and tenderness and faithfulness to her patients. The qualities of a midwife also include strength, diligence, and wisdom, commonly "masculine" characteristics.

Also interesting is the reference to "filthy lucre," which suggests an anxiety over the economics of midwifery. Midwives should conduct themselves out of charity rather than avarice. Of course, the reality is that the very production of a text like *Monument*, as well as *The Byrth of Mankynde* for that matter, originates to some degree in the knowledge that there might be some pecuniary value in the subject matter found in these texts. Male-midwives and physicians had a sense that there was money to be made in delivering babies, and that played some part in the domain of midwifery changing over to men. On the other hand, there is also a sense of the nature of the female birth community in the longing for the midwife to be able to deliver out of charity and to be able to "pleasure all women at all times in my calling." The idea that the midwife has the ability or desire to "give pleasure to, to please, gratify" (*OED,* s.v "pleasure" def. 1) the laboring mother, suggests an intimate relationship between the laboring mother and her midwife and attendants.

This relationship is further imagined in the second and third prayers for midwives where a community of attendants, a midwife, and a laboring woman are defined and controlled. First the midwife asks, as the laboring woman asks in an earlier prayer, for God to "worke thou all our works for us here in secret, that we may praise thy name openlie before all people!" There is both an expression of the birth ritual that takes place in "secret," and an anxiety about the secret ritual. But while this passage brings to mind the famous biblical passage noted above, it also suggests that the work is the work of women, not of God or men. The fact that this secret work is being revealed through the course of this text is both a confirmation of "praising thy name openlie for all people" and an infiltration of that private space.

This intrusion is further confirmed and performed in the last prayer, "In doing hir office, let the midwife praie thus with hir selfe, and saie," which includes three different sections, one of which involves the midwife leading the attending women in prayer. In the course of that section, entitled, "If the woman have verie sore labour, and be long in travelling, and in danger of death, then let the mid-wife, and all the women assistants about hir, kneele downe, and praie one after another, haritlie and earneslie as followeth," the midwife is instructed in how to lead the women in the birth scene through a prayer. This instructional nature of *Monument* can be displayed in the way the text is laid out as dramatic, with the speaker indicated as well as the speech. For example:

> Mid. O Lord save this woman thy servant and hand-maid.
> Wo. Which putteth hir onlie trust in thee.
> Mid. O Lord send hir present helpe from thy holie place.
> Wo. And evermore mightilie defend hir.

> Mid. Let the enimie have none advantage of hir.
> Wo. Nor the wicked approach or hurt hir.
> Mid. Be thou now unto hir, O Lord, a strong tower.
> Wo. From the face of all hir enimies visible and invisible.
> Mid. Lord heare our praiers.
> Wo. And let our crie come unto thee, Amen.[69]

By virtually writing the script for the midwife and female attendants, this directional seeks, more so than in any of the other prayers, to control the nature of the utterances expressed "in secret" to the extent that all of the participants are here delineated. In imagining the extent of female participation in the birth ritual, the text also seeks to define it. That these prayers are written for multiple participants indicates a female community that is imagined and is functioning within the birth community, and that community is in turn defined by the devotional expression of the prayers laid out in the section of Lamp Five.

By bringing together and sometimes conflating spiritual and sacred images with descriptions and experiences of childbirth, the childbirth prayers in *The Monument of Matrones* demonstrate a particular negotiation between the dominant culture's ideas of maternity and female subversion of those ideas indicative of Reformation history. This text shows an intimate relationship between devotional and birth experiences that is a new stage in women's spiritual, psychological, and social lives. These experiences initially seem at odds with one another at the surface level of the text. Through the depiction of these prayers, we can also get a sense of the economy of the dissemination knowledge. The act of publication of a text which is explicitly intended to address female experiences shows an attempt to reveal and, to some degree, control that which is secret: the ritual of birth. But it also indicates the value of what it reveals. This attempt is successful, on the one hand, insofar as men's roles in childbirth practices increased, but was counteracted, on the other hand, by increased female literacy that created an audience for such texts as Jane Sharp's *Midwives Book*, and devotional texts, like *Monument*, designed for female devotional practice.

Notes

PREFACE

¹ See Margaret Ferguson, *Dido's Daughters: Literacy, Gender, and Empire in Early Modern France and England* (Chicago: University of Chicago Press, Forthcoming). See also Frances Dolan, "Reading, Writing, and Other Crimes," from *Feminist Readings of Early Modern Culture: Emerging Subjects*, Valerie Traub, M. Lindsay Kaplan and Dympna Callaghan, eds. (Cambridge: Cambridge University Press, 1996) and Eve Rachele Sanders. *Gender and Literacy on Stage in Early Modern England*. United Kingdom: Cambridge University Press, 1998.

² David Cressy, *Literacy and the Social Order: Reading and Writing in Tudor and Stuart England* (Cambridge: Cambridge University Press, 1980).

³ See R.A.Houston, *Literacy in Early Modern Europe* (London: Longman, 1988), 3. Houston suggests that knowledge and information can be disseminated or obtained in a number of different ways: through looking at an image, through reading either privately or publicly, by attending that which is read either in a small or large, informal or formal groups, and finally, through writing—from a signature to a composition.

⁴ "Scene and Obscene: Seeing and Performing Late Medieval Childbirth," *The Journal of Medieval and Early Modern Studies* 1 (1999): 7–24.

⁵ See for example Monica H Green, *Women's Healthcare in the Medieval West*. Aldershot: Ashgate Publishing Limited, 2000.

⁶ I am indebted to Margaret Ferguson's concept of literacy as a form of cultural capital from *Dido's Daughters: Literacy, Gender, and Empire in Early Modern France and England*.

INTRODUCTION: LITERACY, RITUAL, AND THE REPRODUCTIVE UNCONSCIOUS

¹ While there have been several social and medical histories of medieval notions of sexuality, see especially Joan Cadden, *Meanings of Sex Difference in the Middle Ages: Medicine, Science, and Culture* (Cambridge: Cambridge University Press, 1994), and Danielle Jacquart and Claude Thomasset, *Sexuality and Medicine in the Middle Ages*, trans. Matthew Adamson. (Cambridge: Polity Press, 1988), there have been few examinations of childbirth. Some notable exceptions include David

Cressy's, *Birth, Marriage, and Death: Ritual, Religion, and the Life-Cycle in Tudor and Stuart England* (New York: Oxford University Press, 1997), and Adrian Wilson's, "Participant or Patient? Seventeenth Century Childbirth From the Mother's Point of View," in *Patients and Practitioners. Lay Perceptions of Medicine in Pre-industrial Society*, ed. R. Porter (Cambridge: Cambridge University Press, 1985), pp. 129–44. For a literary analysis that draws childbirth to the center, see Gail McMurray Gibson, "Scene and Obscene: Seeing and Performing Late Medieval Childbirth," *The Journal of Medieval and Early Modern Studies* 29, no. 1 (1999), pp. 7–24. Gibson's article was published after I finished this manuscript, so I do not respond here to her work.

[2] For example, see Sarah Beckwith, *Christ's Body: Identity, Culture, and Society in Late Medieval Writings* (New York: Routledge, 1993), and "A Very Material Mysticism: The Medieval Mysticism of Margery Kempe," in *Medieval Literature: Criticism, Ideology, and History*, ed. David Aers (New York: St. Martin's Press, 1986), pp. 34–57; Caroline Walker Bynum, *Fragmentation and Redemption: Essays on Gender and the Human Body in Medieval Religion* (New York: Zone Books, 1991), and *Holy Feast and Holy Fast: The Religious Significance of Food to Medieval Women* (Berkeley: University of California Press, 1987); Carolyn Dinshaw, *Chaucer's Sexual Poetics* (Madison, WI: University of Wisconsin Press, 1989); *Constructing Medieval Sexuality*, eds. Karma Lochrie, Peggy McCracken, and James A. Schultz (Minneapolis: University of Minnesota Press, 1997); Karma Lochrie, *Margery Kempe and Translations of the Flesh* (Philadelphia: University of Pennsylvania Press, 1991); *Rewriting the Renaissance: The Discourses of Sexual Difference in Early Modern Europe*, eds. Margaret W. Ferguson, Maureen Quilligan, and Nancy J. Vickers (Chicago: University of Chicago Press, 1986); Constance Jordan, *Renaissance Feminism: Literary Texts and Political Models* (Ithaca, NY: Cornell University Press, 1990); Patricia Parker, *Literary Fat Ladies: Rhetoric, Gender, Property* (London; New York: Methuen, 1987), and *"Race," and Writing in the Early Modern Period,* eds. Margo Hendricks and Patricia Parker (NewYork: Routledge, 1994). Also see Judith Butler, *Gender Trouble: Feminism and the Subversion of Identity* (London: Routledge, 1990), and *Bodies That Matter: On the Discursive Limits of "Sex"* (New York: Routledge, 1993).

[3] Texts such as Thomas Laqueur's *Making Sex: Body and Gender from the Greeks to Freud*, (Cambridge, MA: Harvard University Press, 1990), Judith Butler's *Gender Trouble: Feminism and the Subversion of Identity* (New York: Routledge 1990) and *Bodies that Matter* (New York: Routledge, 1993), Louise Fradenburg and Carla Freccero's *Premodern Sexualities* (New York: Routledge, 1996), Domna Stanton's *Discourses of Sexuality: From Aristotle to AIDS* (Ann Arbor: University of Michigan Press, 1992), to name a few, variously take up the question of the nature of sexuality and gender identity and construction and "medical" notions of male and female sexuality.

[4] Fredric Jameson, *The Political Unconscious: Narrative as Socially Symbolic Act* (Ithaca: Cornell University Press, 1981), pp. 75, 95. Also see in particular pp. 81–83. I also take this term "reproductive unconscious" from Patricia Yaeger's essay "The Poetics of Birth," *Discourses of Sexuality* (Ann Arbor: University of Michigan Press, 1992) pp. 262–296. In this essay, Yaeger is interested in the problem of "renarrating birth" as a "central preoccupation of Anglo-American literature"; her interest in the reproductive unconscious is more purely Jamesonian, and

concerned, of course, with nineteenth century production value of labor in childbirth, and the divisions of productive and reproductive labor (287).

[5] Anne Clark Bartlett, *Male Authors, Female Readers: Representation and Subjectivity in Middle English Devotional Literature* (Ithaca: Cornell University Press, 1995), pp. 5–6. Bartlett argues in *Male Authors, Female Readers*, 3–10, that there is more evidence of medieval women's writing and reading practice than has often been claimed, citing documentation of female scribes in the sixth through twelfth centuries and rates of literacy into the sixteenth century that some speculate to be as high as 40%-50% among merchant class men. See also Janet Coleman, *Medieval Readers and Writers, 1350–1400* (London: Hutchinson, 1981), and Margaret W. Ferguson, "A Room Not Their Own: Renaissance Women as Readers and Writers," *The Comparative Perspective on Literature: Approaches to Theory and Practice*, ed. Clayton Koelb (Ithaca. 1988), pp. 93–116.

[6] Brian Stock, *The Implications of Literacy: Written Language and Models of Interpretation in the Eleventh and Twelfth Centuries*, (Princeton: Princeton University Press, 1983) p. 90. Stock is of course is most specifically interested in the role the rise of literacy had in the "formation of heretical and reformist religious groups" (88), and how these groups functioned as textual communities. See also his section on "Textual Communities" pp. 88–240.

[7] See M.T.Clanchy, *From Memory to Written Record: England 1066–1307*, 2nd ed. (Cambridge: Blackwell, 1993), Chapter 7, "Literate and Illiterate," for a more detailed discussion of this issue.

[8] R.A.Houston, *Literacy in Early Modern Europe* (London: Longman, 1988), p. 3. Houston also suggests that knowledge and information can be disseminated or obtained in a number of different ways: through looking at an image, through reading either privately or publicly, by attending that which is read either in a small or large, informal or formal groups, and finally, through writing-from a signature to a composition.

[9] David Cressy, *Literacy and the Social Order: Reading and Writing in Tudor and Stuart England* (Cambridge: Cambridge University Press, 1980), pp. 1–41. See also Nicholas Orme, *Education and Society in Medieval and Renaissance England* (London: Hambledon Press, 1989) for more on education in medieval and early modern England.

[10] See for, example, Rita Copeland, "Rhetoric and the Politics of the Literal Sense in Medieval Literary Theory: Aquinas, Wyclif, and the Lollards," *Rhetoric and Hermeneutics in Our Time: A Reader*, eds. Walter Jost and Michael J. Hyde (New Haven, CT: Yale University Press, 1997), pp. 335–57, and "Rhetoric and Vernacular Translation in the Middle Ages," in *Studies in the Age of Chaucer: The Yearbook of the New Chaucer Society* 9 (1987): 41–75.

[11] As suggested in Michael Van Cleave Alexander's *The Growth of English Education: 1348–1648: A Social and Cultural History* (University Park: Pennsylvania State University Press, 1990), p. 32.

[12] Margery Kempe, for instance, often recalls passages from the Bible as they were read to her. Lollard women are thought to have disseminated long Lollard works through feats of memory—which suggest not only memorization of previously "written" work, but composition of their own original work as well.

[13] Margaret Aston, *Lollards and Reformers: Images and Literacy in Late Medieval Religion* (London: Hambledon Press, 1984), p. 206.

[14] Michael Van Cleave Alexander argues that medieval and early modern women who learned how to read almost always took care to educate their daughters—he cites Elizabeth Woodville and her daughters, and their daughters in turn. He also offers family letters that provide "graphic proof" of the spread of literacy among middle class women (*Growth*, 40).

[15] Bartlett, pp. 6–7. Also see Susan Groag Bell's "Medieval Book Owners: Arbiters of Lay Piety and Ambassadors of Culture," *Signs: Journal of Women in Culture and Society* 7 (1982): 742–68. Reprinted in *Women and Power in the Middle Ages*, eds. Mary Erler and Maryanne Kowaleski (London: University of Georgia Press, 1988), pp. 149–187; and *Sisters and Workers in the Middle Ages*, eds. Judith M. Bennett, Elizabeth A. Clark, Jean F. O'Barr, B. Anne Vilen, and Sarah Westphal-Wihl (Chicago: University of Chicago Press, 1989), pp. 135–161.

[16] That is not to say that nuns and lay women did not use or own texts in Latin or other languages, just that vernacular translations of devotional texts were the more common among these women.

[17] Literacy was essential to the propagation of the Lollard message; so it was therefore not unusual to find men as well as women denying literacy in order to avoid being accused of teaching heretical ideas. For more on this subject, see Anne Hudson, *The Premature Reformation: Wycliffite Texts and Lollard History* (Oxford: Clarendon Press, 1988), and Margaret Aston's *Lollards and Reformers: Images and Literacy in Late Medieval Religion* (London: Hambledon Press, 1984). In addition, Josephine Kosteer Tarvers' essay, "'Thys ys my mystrys boke': English Women as Readers and Writers in Late Medieval England," *The Uses of Manuscripts in Literary Studies: Essays in Memory of Judson Boyce Allen* (Kalamazoo, MI: Western Michigan University, Medieval Institute Publications, 1992), pp. 305–327, refers to several women who were imprisoned for their work spreading the ideas of Wycliffe to their families and Lollard communities, including Alice Dexter, the anchoress Matilda, Anna Palmer, Agnes Nowers, Chirstina More, Agnes Tickhill, Dame Anne Latimer, Dame Alice Sturry, and Katherine Dertford.

[18] See Suzanne W. Hull, *Chaste, Silent and Obedient: English Books for Women, 1475–1640* (San Marino: Huntington Library, 1983), for a comprehensive list and description of books "intended" for women.

[19] In particular, Margaret Roper translated Erasmus' *Precatio Dominica*, or, *Devout Treatese Upon the Pater Noster* (among other now lost translations and compositions). The Cooke sisters (Mildred, Anne, Elizabeth and Katherine) are responsible for several translations, mostly confined to religious material, such as Elizabeth (Cooke) Hoby's *A Way of Reconciliation Touching the True Nature and Substance of the Body and Blood of Christ in the Sacrament*. See Mary Ellen Lamb, "The Cooke Sisters: Attitudes toward Learned Women in the Renaissance," *Silent But for the Word: Tudor Women as Patrons, Translators, and Writers of Religious Works*, ed., Hannay, pp.105–125.

[20] John N. King, "Patronage and Piety: The Influence of Catherine Parr," *Silent But for the Word*, ed. Hannay, p. 43. Catherine Parr herself published her original work, *Prayers or Medytacions* (1546) and *Lamentation of a Sinner* (1545), in an affordable form, addressed it to women, and intended it for use as a supplement to the Bible.

[21] Bartlett argues this scenario specifically in the use of devotional texts, but this construct can be applied to any number of texts used by women (20–21).

CHAPTER ONE. "I WYL WRIGHT OF WOMEN PREVY SEKENESSE": FEMALE TEXTUAL AND BIRTH COMMUNITIES AND THE HISTORY OF WOMEN'S MEDICAL TEXTS

[1] Medieval and early modern understanding of male and female physiology did not change substantially from the ancients.

[2] Beginning in the later sixteenth century, and more commonly in the seventeenth century, practitioners also followed and/or mixed their humoral-based practice with Paracelsian methods (which preferred chemical remedies). For more on Paracelsus, see Allen G. Debus, *The Chemical Philosophy: Paracelsian Science and Medicine in the Sixteenth and Seventeenth Centuries* (New York: Science History Publications, 1977).

[3] For a thorough discussion of theories of the humors, see Joan Cadden, *Meanings of Sex Difference in the Middle Ages: Medicine, Science, and Culture* (Cambridge: Cambridge University Press, 1994), and Danielle Jacquart and Claude Thomasset, *Sexuality and Medicine in the Middle Ages*, trans. Matthew Adamson. (Cambridge: Polity Press, 1988).

[4] See Laqueur, *Making Sex*, particularly Chapters Two and Three.

[5] This condition is a result of multiple births and the weakening of the muscles that hold the uterus in place; it was likely a fairly common ailment given that medieval and early modern women often had many children—it was not unusual for a woman to have eight. See Beryl Rowland, *Medieval Woman's Guide to Health* (Kent State University Press, 1981), p. 97, for the description of the treatment of a prolapsed uterus.

[6] As quoted in Elizabeth Robertson, "Medieval Medical Views of Women and Female Spirituality in the *Ancrene Wisse* and Julian of Norwich's *Showings*." *Feminist Approaches to the Body in Medieval Literature*," eds. Linda Lomperis and Sarah Stanbury (Philadelphia: University of Pennsylvania, 1993), p. 144.

[7] See Joan Cadden, *Meanings of Sex Difference in the Middle Ages* (Cambridge: Cambridge University Press, 1993), pp. 94–5, 143; and see also Carol Rawcliffe, *Medicine & Society in Later Medieval England* (United Kingdom: Alan Sutton Publishing, 1995), p. 174, in which Rawcliffe writes, "Since it was widely understood that conception required the emission of female as well as male semen, and that the former could only be produced in response to pleasure, theologians drew the obvious conclusions: if a woman became pregnant, even when raped, her baser, animal nature must have overwhelmed her moral sense." It seems unlikely that a woman who became pregnant after being raped would agree with this theory.

[8] See for example, Saint Augustine, *Concerning the City of God Against the Pagans*, trans. H Bettenson (Harmondsworth, Middlesex: Penguin Books, 1984), Saint Jerome, *Select Letters of St. Jerome*, trans. F.A. Wright. (Cambridge: Harvard University Press, 1980), Saint Bonaventure, *The Journey of the Mind to God*, trans. Philotheus Boehner, ed. Stephen F. Brown (Indianapolis: Hackett Publishing, 1993).

[9] Rowland, p. 58.

[10] A list of works includes William Sermon, *The Ladies Companion, or the English Midwife* (1671), Hugh Chamberlen's translation of *The Diseases of Women with Child* (1672, 1683), and *The Accomplisht Midwife* (1673) by Francis Mauriceau, W.M. and Hannah Woolley, *The Queens Closet Opened* (1674), and *The Gentlewoman's Companion* (1675), *The English Midwife Enlarged* (1682), John Pechey, *A General Treatise of the Diseases of Maids, Big-Bellied Women, Child-bed Women, and Widows* (1696).

[11] See Merry E. Wiesner, "Early Modern Midwifery," p. 31.

[12] *The Ladies Companion, or, The English Midwife: Wherein is Demonstrated the Manner and Order How Women Ought to Govern Themselves During the Whole Time of their Breeding Children and of their Difficult Labour* (London: Printed for Edward Thomas, 1671); Percival Willughby, *Observations in Midwifery* (Warwick, 1863; Wakefield, 1972). He was assisted apparently by one of his two daughters, Miss Willughby, in the 1650s. Not much is known of her except that she assisted her father.

[13] *The Diary of Ralph Josselin*, ed. A. Macfarlane (London, 1976).

[14] I use this general material as it was put together by and found in the work of Adrian Wilson and David Cressy. See also Adrian Wilson's "The Ceremony of Childbirth and its Interpretation," *Women as Mothers in Pre-Industrial England: Essays in Memory of Dorothy McLaren*, ed. Valerie Fideles (London and New York: Routledge, 1990). David Cressy also argues that while there was an explosion of texts on the subject of "the business of childbirth, yet many of the day-to-day secrets of the birthroom remained behind the veil," *Birth, Marriage and Death*, p. 39.

[15] The image is divided into three parts. The first part shows a woman in bed after delivery with a midwife by her side, offering a basin with a spoon in it; a woman standing by a fire warming a towel, and one attending the baby in a cradle. The second part shows a christening in which the midwife is walking in front of a processional with the child. The third image is of a christening feast, with women sitting around the table having wine, etc. with the parson most prominent.

[16] There are also clues to be found in the diaries and autobiographies of women such as Lady Grace Mildmay, Anne Thornton, and Lady Anne Hoby.

[17] Wilson, "Participant," p. 94.

[18] See Arnold Van Gennep, *The Rites of Passage*, trans. M.B. Vizedome and G.L. Caffee (London, 1960), pp. 10–11, 46. As quoted in Adrian Wilson, "Participant," p. 141.

[19] See for example *Diary of Lady Hoby*, ed. Dorothy Meades (Boston and New York: Houghton Mifflin Company, 1930), pp. 72, 86, 100, 101, 184, in which Lady Hoby describes variously attending her sister in childbirth, and her mother attending her in childbirth.

[20] As quoted from M.J. Tucker, "The Child as Beginning and End: Fifteenth- and Sixteenth-Century English Childhood," *The History of Childhood*, ed. Lloyd deMause (New York: Harper and Row, 1975), p. 238.

[21] Wilson acknowledges that Josselin's evidence on this is fragmented, but the order seems to be consistent from description to description nonetheless.

[22] There is some suggestion (from very limited evidence) that sexual relations were to be abstained from until the lying-in period was over. It should be noted as well that the whole confinement process is related to the general ability of a woman to recover from childbirth, which was marked by the ceremony of churching, and that there are similar "guidelines" practiced in the recovery process today. In theory the mother could not go outside until she was churched, or purified.

[23] Women of the upper classes seemed to be more likely to participate in the ritual that Wilson outlines than lower-class women, although there is no real way of knowing. The main difference appears not to be who attended the birth (in terms of numbers of women), but rather the length of the ritual; lower-class women were more likely to leave the chamber, and be seen by men (husband, then relatives, then

Notes to Chapter One

priest and public) sooner than their upper-class counterparts. In addition, the enclosed space might be limited to the bed and not a whole room, and such a woman might have had her baby at a person's house that was larger than her own.

[24] Wilson, "Participant," p. 78.

[25] Ibid., p. 79.

[26] See, Monica Green, "Obstetrical and Gynecological Texts," *Studies in the Age of Chaucer* 14 (1992), pp. 54.

[27] There are, of course, many different kinds of texts that relate to the issue of women's health, ranging from theoretical models based on contemporary medical physician's translations, transcriptions, interpretations and readings of Latin medical texts based on Galen, etc., to the more practical medicinal recipes for easy delivery. While these texts are important to the history of the female reproductive body, a comprehensive discussion of them is a task beyond the scope of this project. One very popular text that I don't take up here at any length is the late-thirteenth or early-fourteenth century Pseudo-Albertus Magnus' *De Secretis Mulierum*.

[28] See Wendy Arons: *When Midwifery Became the Male Physician's Province: The Sixteenth Century Handbook: The Rose Garden for Pregnant Women and Midwives Newly Englished* (Jefferson, North Carolina: McFarland & Company, 1994).

[29] See John F. Benton, "Trotula, Women's Problems, and the Professionalization of Medicine in the Middle Ages," *Bulletin of the History of Medicine* 59 (1985), pp. 30–53.

[30] Benton, p. 41.

[31] For one of the many accounts of "dangerous" midwives see J.H. Aveling, *English Midwives: Their History and Prospects* (London: AMS Press, 1872).

[32] For example, Chaucer includes *Trotula* in the Wife of Bath's catalogue of Jenkyn's book of "wicked wives," in *The Prologue to the Wife of Bath's Tale*, from *The Canterbury Tales*, *The Riverside Chaucer*, 3rd ed., ed. F.N. Robinson (Boston: Houghton Mifflin, 1987), pp. 114, 666–681.

[33] Karma Lochrie, *Covert Operations: The Medieval Uses of Secrecy* (Philadelphia: University of Pennsylvania Press, 1999), p. 8.

[34] Rowland, *Medieval Woman's Guide to Health*.

[35] In fact, there is only very little of the *Trotula* text in Rowland's translation; those sections which are from the *Trotula* have to do with the treatment of a prolapsed uterus, a cure for a windy uterus, and the promotion of conception. See Monica Green, "Obstetrical and Gynecological Texts," p. 73.

[36] See Monica Green, "Obstetrical and Gynecological Texts," p. 56.

[37] Over three dozen of the 118 extant Latin versions in Europe were apparently copied in England, according to Green in "Obstetrical and Gynecological Texts," p. 64.

[38] British Library Additional 12195, fol.157r-v, as quoted by Monica Green, "Obstetrical and Gynecological Texts," p. 65.

[39] I am thinking of a variety of texts in which gossips are represented such as the *Noah* play in the *Wakefield* Cycle Drama, the description of the "outer rule" in the *Ancrene Wisse*, to name but two.

[40] Green notes that the title "Sekenesse of Wymmen" is not used consistently in the manuscripts, but is her own reference. Other titles include: "Sores and greuance that wommen have," "The secreate diseasys of women," "Liber Tepucreseos Galieni" and "Liber Trotularis," "Obstectrical and Gynelogical Texts," pp. 77–8.

41 Rowland, p. 58.
42 Ibid., p. 59.
43 Green, "Obstetrical and Gynecological Texts," p. 77.
44 Jesus College 43, fol.70v., as quoted by Green in "Obstetrical," p. 71.
45 Cressy notes that "childbirth manuals plagiarized unmercifully and repeated each other's venerable observations," *Birth, Marriage and Death: Ritual, Religion, and the Life-Cycle in Tudor and Stuart England* (Oxford: Oxford University Press, 1997), p. 36.
46 See Merry Weisner, "Early Modern Midwives: A Case Study," *International Journal of Women's Studies* 6(1) (1983), p. 28.
47 Arons, p. 32.
48 Ibid., p. 33.
49 Ibid., p. 34.
50 Weisner, p. 32.
51 Arons, p. 35.
52 See Weisner, pp. 26–43. In this article Weisner suggests the methods by which midwives generally kept their information to themselves.
53 According to Ballantyne, Thomas Raynald was a printer in St Paul's Churchyard, London, and printed several books between the years 1540 and 1555, including two editions of *Byrth* (1540 and 1545), a *Treatise against the Masse* (1548), a *Plaister for a Galled Horse* (1548), the *Boke of Barthra Priest* (1549), *Certain Psalmes*, Thomas Wyatt (1549) and a folio *Byble* (1549). Thomas Raynald, the Physician, is apparently responsible for several additions to the *Byrth* in subsequent editions (including anatomical illustrations).
54 Ballantyne cites this inscription on page 321. Also, see Ballantyne, pp. 302–3, where he quotes from the text: "Wherefore now to come to our purpose, ye schal understand that about thre or foure yeres past, a certayne studious and diligent clarke, at the request and desyre of diuvers and honest matrones, beynge of hys acquayntaunce, dyd translate out of Latin into English a great part of thys boke, entiteling it according to the Latine inscription (de partu hominis, that is to saye: of the byrth of mankynd) which we nowe do name (The womans boke) (for so moch as the most parte or well neare all therein entreated of, doth concerne and touche onely women)."
55 It would be interesting to investigate the reasons why the more realistic and accurate anatomical figures included in the 1560 edition were not included in all of the later editions.
56 See Green, "Obstetrical and Gynecological Texts," p. 58.
57 See Adrian Wilson, "Participant or Patient? Seventeenth Century Childbirth from the Mother's Point of View," *Patients and Practitioners: Lay Perceptions of Medicine in Pre-industrial Society* (Cambridge: Cambridge University Press, 1985), pp. 129–144. For more on the male move into childbirth management, see Jean Donnison, *Midwives and Medical Men: A History of Interprofessional Rivalries and Women's Rights* (New York: Schocken Books, 1977) and Arons in her Introduction to *Rose Garden*, pp. 2–27. Arons suggests that there were many factors involved in the gradual shift of midwives attending women in birth to the employment of male-midwives and physicians in the mid-seventeenth century.
58 Ballantyne, p. 308. For a thorough description and treatment of all editions, see Ballantyne, pp. 307–325.

⁵⁹ It is not exactly clear, however, which Catherine the text refers to; Catherine of Aragon was annulled in May 1533, Henry married Catherine Howard in 1540 (and had her beheaded in 1542), it is assumed this is who *Byrth* is dedicated to, as he married Catherine Parr in 1543.

⁶⁰ *Byrth*, fol. C viii.

⁶¹ See, for example, Thomas Laqueur, *Making Sex*. I, like many scholars, have some problems with accepting the single-sex theory as a practical approach by contemporary practitioners and/or midwives.

⁶² Ballantyne, p. 313.

⁶³ to to, MS, i.e., top to toe.

⁶⁴ *Byrth*, Bi.

⁶⁵ *Byrth*, Biii.

⁶⁶ This passage is longer and differs somewhat from later editions in which Raynald calls for women to follow the instructions in his book, but does not go into length about the possible places women have used a text such as this.

⁶⁷ *Byrth*, Cii.

CHAPTER TWO: THEOLOGIZED MATERNITY IN JULIAN OF NORWICH'S *BOOK OF SHOWINGS*

¹ *The Book of Margery Kempe*, EETS o.s. 212, ed. Sanford Brown Meech (London: Oxford University Press, 1940), p. 41.

² *The Book of Margery Kempe*, p. 43.

³ B.A. Windeatt in his modern edition of *The Book of Margery Kempe* translates dalliance rather over simply as "holy conversation." See *The Book of Margery Kempe*, trans. B.A. Windeatt (Penguin Books 1985), p. 78.

⁴ I use *A Book of Showings to the Anchoress Julian of Norwich*, Parts 1 and 2, eds. Edmund Colledge and James Walsh (Toronto: Pontifical Institute of Medieval Studies, 1978).

⁵ See the introductions to *Julian of Norwich: A Revelation of Love*, ed. Marion Glascoe (University of Exeter, 1976), and *A Book of Showings to the Anchoress Julian of Norwich*, Parts 1&2, eds. Edmund Colledge and James Walsh (Toronto: Pontifical Institute of Medieval Studies, 1978) and Georgia Ronan Crampton, *The Shewings of Julian of Norwich* (Kalamazoo: Medieval Institute Publications, 1994). There are three extant full manuscripts, commonly known as Paris, BN MS fonds anglais 40 (P), BL MS Sloane 2499 (S1) and BL MS Sloane 3705 (S2); none of these manuscripts is from earlier than the seventeenth century. Manuscript P appears to be from about 1650, as does S1. S2 appears to be in an eighteenth-century hand, with further modernized spellings. While P is more modernized and "clean" (Colledge and Walsh use this version), Glascoe argues that S1 comes closer to Julian's fourteenth-century language (Glascoe, viii), and Crampton suggests that while "the Sloane scribe [S1] may indeed have shortened the copy text...it is also possible that the Paris [P] scribe amplified" (Crampton, 22).

⁶ Carolyn Walker Bynum in particular has addressed the complexity of medieval notions of the body, particularly the female mystical experience, in her books *Holy Feast and Holy Fast: The Religious Significance of Food to Medieval Women* (Berkeley: University of California Press, 1987) and *Fragmentation and Redemption: Essays on Gender and the Human Body in Medieval Religion* (New York: Zone Books, 1991). More recently, Karma Lochrie, in her book *Margery*

Kempe and Translations of the Flesh (Philadelphia: University of Pennsylvania Press, 1991), has done significant work in complicating our understanding of medieval notions of the body by arguing that women were in particular associated with the flesh, which was often denigrated, whereas the body might escape these denigrations. Likewise, Sarah Beckwith's *Christ's Body: Identity, Culture, and Society in Late Medieval Writings* (London: Routledge, 1993) explores the relationship of the female mystical body to the culture. Elizabeth Robertson in particular takes up the specific relationship between medical views of women and the practice and representations of their spiritual experience in her essay "Medieval Medical Views of Women and Female Spirituality in the *Ancrene Wisse* and Julian of Norwich's *Showings*," in *Feminist Approaches to the Body in Medieval Literature*, eds. Linda Lomperis and Sarah Stanbury (Philadelphia: University of Pennsylvania Press, 1993), pp. 142–167.

[7] Robertson, "Medieval Medical Views," p. 142.

[8] E.J. Dobson, *The Origins of the Ancrene Wisse* (Oxford, England: Clarendon Press, 1976).

[9] Elizabeth Robertson, *Early English Devotional Prose and the Female Audience* (Knoxville: University of Tennessee Press, 1990), p. 2.

[10] Robertson, *Early English Devotional Prose*, p. 3.

[11] Robertson argues that there were more women who desired to become anchorites in the twelfth and thirteenth century than in earlier periods, a fact that comes out of the Norman appropriation of Anglo-Saxon convents. Robertson also argues that "these women had a complex relationship to the Christian tradition: while firmly embedded within it, they were denied access to positions of authority; they were dependent on visiting priests for confession; and they had little or no training in Latin" (8). However, their enclosure meant that they were discouraged from worldly activities and work, so they spent a lot of time reading, and these texts have been rather limited.

[12] All quotations are from *Hali Meidenhad*, EETS, no.18, ed. F.J. Furnivall (New York: Greenwood Press, 1969), p. 2.

[13] All translations are mine unless otherwise noted.

[14] *Hali Meidenhad*, pp. 32–34.

[15] Ibid., p. 46.

[16] Ibid., p. 49.

[17] Translation from *Medieval English Prose for Women, Selections from the Katherine Group and the* Ancrene Wisse, eds. Bella Millet and Jocelyn Wogan-Browne (Oxford: Clarendon Press, 1990), pp. 30–33.

[18] All quotations are from *Ancrene Wisse*, EETS, no. 249, ed. J.R.R. Tolkien (London: Oxford University Press, 1962), pp. 211–12.

[19] Millet and Wogan-Browne, p. 133.

[20] In contrast, a recluse "ne schulen habbe na beast bute cat ane" (should have no beast but a cat), because to have livestock means having to be preoccupied with their behavior. *Ancrene Wisse*, p. 213.

[21] Ibid., pp. 32–33.

[22] Ibid., p. 35.

[23] Ibid., p. 35.

[24] Ibid., p. 35.

[25] Ibid., p. 218.

[26] Ibid., p. 218.

27 This is in contrast to Margery, who avidly insists on her own material existence in *The Book of Margery Kempe*. For a thorough discussion of this see Sarah Beckwith's essay, "A Very Material Mysticism: The Medieval Mysticism of Margery Kempe," in David Aers, *Medieval Literature: Criticism, Ideology, and History*. New York: St. Martin's Press, 1986.

28 See, for example, Andrew Sprung, "The Inverted Metaphor: Earthly Mothering as Figura of Divine Love in Julian of Norwich's *Book of Showings*," in *Medieval Mothering*, eds. John Carmi Parsons and Bonnie Wheeler (New York: Garland, 1996), pp. 183–211. Sprung argues in this psychoanalytic reading of Julian's text that she is interested in casting God as the perfect mother, and that for Julian God is our "true" and "perfect" mother, whereas our earthly mothers "are imperfect figura of God's absolute nurturance" (183).

29 Pamela Sheingorn, in her essay "The Maternal Behavior of God: Divine Father as Fantasy Husband," in *Medieval Mothering*, argues that the identification of God with attributes of mothering "shared in the construction of His masculinity even as it communicated an image of male tenderness and attentive concern." This, in turn, "buttressed normative heterosexuality and female submissiveness" (77).

30 The representation of older "maternal" men caring for younger women suggests a desire on these women's part to be cared for (mothered) by these older men; it was also a way to make culturally more acceptable (and desirable) the marriage of younger women to older men.

31 Maud Burnett McInerney, "In the Meydens Womb: Julian of Norwich and the Poetics of Enclosure," *Medieval Mothering*, 157–82.

32 Colledge and Walsh, p. 285.

33 Ibid., p. 291.

34 Ibid., p. 290–2.

35 Like Margery Kempe's text in the opening chapters, Julian's Chapter 3 describes the bodily illness as a near death one that moved her to take her last rites.

36 Julian also focuses on the Passion and Christ's pain as a kind of labor: "and in this fallyng he toke grete soore. The soore that he toke was oure flesshe, in whych as sone he had felyng of dedely paynes" (Colledge and Walsh, 540). Also, while not speaking to labor in childbirth specifically, Elaine Scarry argues that the experience of pain precludes language. See Elaine Scarry, *The Body in Pain: The Making and the Unmaking of the World* (Oxford: Oxford University Press, 1985).

37 Colledge and Walsh, p. 293.

38 Robertson, p. 154.

39 "Ony mene" in Crampton's edition, p. 43.

40 Colledge and Walsh, p. 294.

41 Roberston, "Medical Views," p. 154. The purging of excess humors could also apply to Margery, whose excessive crying could be seen as a means to rid her of her excess moisture and in order to restore her to a more perfect "dry" state.

42 Some may argue that she becomes more "alive" as she enters her revelatory state.

43 Colledge and Walsh, p. 311.

44 Robertson, "Medical Views," p. 157.

45 Colledge and Walsh, pp. 292–3.

46 McInerney, p. 154.

47 Colledge and Walsh, p. 619.

48 Ibid., p. 619.

⁴⁹ As Colledge and Walsh note, "this is the only occasion when a 'bodily sight' is described which is not already reported in the short text" (622, n.31).

⁵⁰ Ibid., pp. 622–3.

⁵¹ Robertson's "Medieval Views" (142–167) suggests medical notions of women can be seen in Julian's text in the form of images of menstruation.

⁵² Colledge and Walsh, p. 623, n.32.

⁵³ The word "swylge" seems to be a (perhaps vagrant) version of "swilg." Also, see Colledge and Walsh, p. 622.

⁵⁴ Crampton, p. 130.

⁵⁵ Ibid., p. 195.

⁵⁶ Colledge and Walsh, pp. 622–3.

⁵⁷ Ibid., pp. 623–4.

⁵⁸ Karma Lochrie's *Margery Kempe and Translations of the Flesh*.

⁵⁹ This works in contrast to, as well as parallel to, an interesting moment in Chapter 55, Revelation 14, which offers an example of Julian "theologizing maternity." Here, Julian describes the "birth" of our soul, what she refers to "oure furst makyng," or our Creation: "And what tyme oure soule is enspyred in oure body, in whych we be made sensuall, as soone mercy and grace begin to werke...(566). Here "enspyred" is breathing.

⁶⁰ *Hali Meidenhad*, p. 33.

⁶¹ These anxieties are borne out in texts like the sixteenth-century *Monument of Matrones*, in which women despair over seeming endless labors. See my Chapter 4.

⁶² Colledge and Walsh, p. 580.

⁶³ Even her description of how the vision came to her suggests a desire for the metaphorical womb: "Plentuously, fully and swetely was this shewde; and it is spoken of in the furst, wher it seyde we be all in hym beclosyd, and he beclosyd in vs" (580).

CHAPTER THREE: A VERY MATERNAL MYSTICISM: IMAGES OF CHILDBIRTH AND ITS RITUALS IN *THE BOOK OF MARGERY KEMPE*

¹ My title plays off the title of Sarah Beckwith's important essay "A Very Material Mysticism: The Medieval Mysticism of Margery Kempe," in *Medieval Literature: Criticism, Ideology and History*, ed. David Aers (Brighton: Harvester, 1986), pp. 34–57, and *Gender and Text in the Later Middle Ages*, ed. Jane Chance (Gainesville: University Press of Florida, 1996), pp. 195–215.

² I use *The Book of Margery Kempe*, EETS, no. 212, eds. Hope Emily Allen and Sanford Brown Meech (London: Oxford University Press, 1940).

³ Hope Phyllis Weissman argues that Margery manipulates the standard model of a saint's life, which includes a narrative that recounts the saint's childhood and rehearses "a tale of persecutions and triumphs," bypassing the description of childhood, and moving right to her marriage and childbed, thereby subverting the standard form. "Margery Kempe in Jerusalem: Hysterica Compassio in the Late Middle Ages," in *Acts of Interpretation: The Text in its Contexts 700–1600*, eds. Mary J.Carruthers and Elizabeth D. Kirk (Norman:Pilgrim, 1982), pp. 210–217.

⁴ Wendy Harding, "Medieval Women's Unwritten Discourse on Motherhood: A Reading of Two Fifteenth-Century Texts," in *Women's Studies: An Interdisciplinary Journal* 21, no. 2 (1992), pp. 197–209.

⁵ Carolyn Walker Bynum has famously suggested that "Margery, for all her fervor, her courage, her piety, cannot write her own script." Bynum, *Fragmentation and Redemption: Essays on Gender and the Human Body in Medieval Religion* (New York: Zone, 1991), p. 41. Beckwith argues in her conclusion to her very important essay, "A Very Material Mysticism," that Margery in "misrecognizing herself in him [Christ], by living a life which is itself a mimesis and remembrance of the Passion...is a strategy that never attempts, that is unable to attempt, to break the mold of its subjection. Indeed it cannot, for it is the very equation of victimization, passivity, subjection with femininity, that allows the Christian inversion its paradoxical triumph" (54). Karma Lochrie, while seeing Margery's text as finally enabling her voice, argues that the process of "intruding" into written culture ultimately leads to alienation from her own; and the mystic text, always unstable, is situated "both within the authorized institution of the Church and outside it." *Margery Kempe and Translations of the Flesh* (Philadelphia: University of Pennsylvania Press, 1991), p. 122.

⁶ Caroline Walker Bynum, "The Female Body and Religious Practice in the Later Middle Ages," *Fragments for a History of the Human Body*, eds. Michel Feher with Ramona Naddaff and Nadia Tazi (New York: Zone, 1989), p. 200.

⁷ Gail McMurray Gibson, *The Theater of Devotion: East Anglian Drama and Society in the Late Middle Ages* (Chicago: University of Chicago Press, 1989), p. 50.

⁸ See Gibson's *The Theater of Devotion*, in which she argues that Margery's practices are an "extremely literal and concrete achievement of those very spiritual exercises" of the thirteenth-century writer of the *Mediationes vitae Christi* (49).

⁹ Harding, "Unwritten," p. 198.

¹⁰ Kaplan, p. 40.

¹¹ See Elaine Scarry, *The Body in Pain* (Oxford: Oxford University Press, 1985), p. 4.

¹² Lawrence Stone, *Family, Sex, and Marriage In England 1500–1800* (London: Harper Torchbooks, 1977), p. 53.

¹³ David Cressy, *Birth, Marriage, and Death: Ritual, Religion, and The Life-Cycle in Tudor and Stuart England*, p. 30. See also Patricia Crawford, *Women as Mothers in Pre-Industrial England*.

¹⁴ Harding, "Unwritten," p. 204. Not being pregnant also was cause for anxiety. A woman who did not become pregnant in her marriage had a great deal of stress, for to be barren was considered a curse (by God), and to be fruitful was considered a blessing.

¹⁵ *The Book of Margery Kempe*, p. 6.

¹⁶ It is also at this moment that Margery figures birth as a rare means of production (this happens later in the text as well at the births of Mary, John the Baptist, and Christ). Women's labor in birth was not associated with or equal to the kinds of labor and production of men. In this sense, all production is unequal between men and women. Of course, without the "production" of children, there can be no other kinds of production, and yet reproduction is reduced to a lower status. See Patricia Yaeger, "Poetics of Birth," in which she argues that those who labor (work) are historically set up in opposition to those who reproduce (women who labor), p. 95.

¹⁷ *The Book of Margery Kempe*, p. 6–7.

[18] *The Book of Margery Kempe*, p. 7. It seems as if doing penance by herself, Lollard in its essence, is acceptable to one group in the culture, but a ritual among women is not. Margery is often accused of Lollardy in her text—as when she is arrested by the Mayor of Leicester (111ff)—and, not insignificantly, Lollard practices were equated with threatening lay literacy, female lay literacy, and female textual communities. See Ann Hudson, *The Premature Reformation: Wycliffite texts and Lollard History* (Oxford [Oxfordshire]: Clarendon Press, 1988).

[19] *The Book of Margery Kempe*, p. 7.

[20] Gibson also asserts that "there are moments in *The Book of Margery Kempe* when the magic of popular rituals of conception and childbed and the practices of Christian devotion seem inseparable" (62).

[21] *The Book of Margery Kempe*, p. 7.

[22] *The Book of Margery Kempe*, p. 7. Margery later has a parallel moment when, in Chapter 75, she symbolically recreates her own madness after birth. A man comes to her while she is praying in the church of St. Margaret and when Margery inquires into his distress, he says that his wife was "newly delyueryd of a childe & sche was owt hir mende. '&, dame,' he seyth, 'sche knowyth not mene non of hir newborwys. Sche roryth & cryith so þat sche makit folk euyl a-feerd'" (177–178). Margery goes to her side and comforts her, stays with her, and visits once or twice a day (as she was bound and chained so as not to hurt anyone) until she recovers, at which point she is reintgrated into society: "and þan was sche browt to chirche & purifijd as oþer women be, blyssed mote God ben" (178). Margery, it seems, has restored the woman to reason, as she herself is restored to reason in this passage by Christ. Gibson argues that this is a kind of "healing" in which Margery "has extended the incarnational likeness" (65) of Christ, thereby coming full circle and, as I have argued in other places, sets herself up as a key player in sacred history and narrative.

[23] *The Book of Margery Kempe*, p. 8.

[24] Sandra McEntire argues that this moment of reason "marks the beginning of her awakening of her new self, one identified with the godhead...Kempe's awakening and subjectivity to new spiritual possibilities are grounded not in repression and punishment of her body...but in spiritualizing and affirming female bodily nurturing" (58–9). As McEntire notes, while Margery "wakes" here to the power and notion of godhead with renewed strength, and possibly as heightened sense of "self," the affirmation of "female bodily nurturing" does not come without ambivalence and ambiguities. See "The Journey into Selfhood: Margery Kempe and Feminine Spirituality" in *Margery Kempe: A Book of Essays* (New York: Garland Press, 1992), pp. 51–69.

[25] Weissman, p. 211.

[26] *The Book of Margery Kempe*, p. 17.

[27] Harding, "Unwritten," p. 206.

[28] For a discussion of the image of the infantilized Christ, see David Aers, *Community, Gender and Individual Identity: English Writing 1360–1430* (London and New York: Routledge, 1988), 107, Sarah Beckwith (48) and Kathy Lavezzo, "Sobs and Sighs Between Women: The Homoerotics of Compassion in *The Book of Margery Kempe*," in *Premodern Sexualities*, eds. Louise Fradenburg and Carla Freccero (New York: Routledge, 1996), p. 181.

[29] *The Book of Margery Kempe*, p. 18.

[30] Lavezzo makes this point in relation to Margery as well, p. 185.

[31] *The Book of Margery Kempe*, p. 18.

[32] Sarah Beckwith in her essay discusses Margery Kempe's materialism not so much specifically to the role of parenthood, but more generally to Margery's material insistence in her construction of "femininity and subjectivity" (34) through her relationship in God incarnate, Christ. In "A Very Material Mysticism" Beckwith talks about positive mysticism (which makes up part of what she calls "material" mysticism) and negative mysticism. Positive mysticism "uses imagery and analogy to approximate and approach God, seeing the Incarnation as the type and legitimation of such symbolising, the means through which God descends, and reciprocally the means of mystical ascent to God" (38). Negative mysticism on the other hand "abjures all symbol which it sees as necessarily inadequate; God's divinity being without limit, he cannot be finitely enclosed within any analogy or symbol, but only by the mystics' kenosis or self-emptying..." (39). Even though there is a spectrum, many female mystics are associated with "negative" mysticism, like Julian, while some, like Margery, are associated more with the "positive."

[33] The description of Mary's clothing in this chapter is reminiscent of Margery's own manner of dress on several occasions. See chapters 17 and 23, where Margery dresses all in white like the Virgin, under the instruction of Christ, and later where she is herself dressed by others in white.

[34] *The Book of Margery Kempe*, p. 18. Later, Margery rehearses the Annunciation, only this time she is the recipient (she situates herself as Mary) of the word from Christ: "In þe tyme þat þis creatur had reuelacyons, owyr Lord seyd to hir, "Dowtyr, þow art wyth childe." Sche seyd a- en, "A, Lord, how xal I þan do for kepyn of my chylde?" Owir Lord seyd, "Dowtyr, drede þe not, I xal ordeyn for an kepar" (48). As they go on to talk about whether she is worthy to talk to Christ (as she isn't a virgin or chaste), he explains how he loves her no matter what, essentially blessing her procreative activities: "I wyl þat þow bryng me forth more frwte."

[35] *The Book of Margery Kempe*, p. 18.

[36] In Julian of Norwich's *Book of Showings*, Julian comes to understand Mary in Chapter 4, Revelation 1, in similar terms as Margery's. She sees Mary as "ghostly in bodily lykenes, a simple mayden and a meeke, yong of age, a little waxen aboue a chylde, in the same stature as she was when she conceivede" (297). There is attention to the "conception" of Christ as a conception, but, like Kempe's text, her pregnancy and birth is elided.

[37] Maternity gets elided in all different genres of medieval and early modern texts (in Cycle Plays, in Chaucer) as a response to men's and women's anxieties over birth. The Virgin (Mary) who remains intact and is the holy vessel, and then later becomes revered by women, is of course the supreme model of this elision.

[38] *The Book of Margery Kempe*, p. 18.

[39] Gibson tells us that there is a fragmentary recipe that appears on the verso of the last folio of the Kempe manuscript, and suggests that "it would not be surprising if...[it] was intended to be the recipe for Margery's wine caudle" (51).

[40] *The Book of Margery Kempe*, p. 19.

[41] Although not one who doubts, as is sometimes the case.

[42] *The Book of Margery Kempe*, p. 19.

[43] Ibid., p. 19.

[44] Ibid., p. 19.

[45] This conflation of Margery with Mary, as well as the conflation of her duties with that of Joseph, testifies to Margery's complex relationship to her own mater-

nity and to the ideas of paternity and authorship, a discussion of which goes beyond the scope of this chapter.

[46] In fact, as Bynum notes, some theorists of conception like Galen feared that if women were supplied the "matter" as well as the form "she might impregnate herself and the male would have no role at all...this threatens the importance of the male contribution to life." "Female Body," p. 214.

[47] Ibid., p. 77.

[48] As Kathy Lavezzo points out, it was not uncommon for women to focus their spiritual reveries on the image of the Christ-child. Lavezzo does a wonderfully nuanced reading of the Christ doll episode in which she argues that the passivized doll enables female homoeroticism. See Kathy Lavezzo, pp. 184–187.

[49] Gibson, p. 63.

[50] Lavezzo argues this in particular relation to Margery Kempe and the Worshipful Wives' active (erotic) mourning over the Christ doll, in which "...the power the Christic object represents is not intrinsic to itself, but is, rather, conferred upon it by the women...the women resignify his body as object for their own desiring ends" (190).

[51] *The Book of Margery Kempe*, pp. 77–78.

[52] Ibid., p. 78.

[53] Ibid., p. 17.

[54] Ibid., p. 78.

[55] Lavezzo, p. 186.

[56] Weissman, p. 215.

[57] This is claimed in the Introductions to the *Book* in both *The Norton Anthology of Literature by Women*, ed. Gilbert and Gubar (New York: Norton, 1985), p. 21, and in *The Norton Anthology of English Literature*, Vol. 1. 6th edition, ed. Abrams, et. al. (New York: Norton). Further, it has been considered autobiographical (rather than devotional in the way that Julian of Norwich's work is) because of Margery's involvement in the world.

[58] In fact, there were two men to whom she dictated her life, a German gentleman and the Priest who ends up transcribing and scribing Margery's life. For a description of how her *Book* came to be written see Allen, pp. 3–5.

[59] It is likely that Margery was illiterate in the modern sense of the word, but, as many scholars such as Brian Stock, Anne Bartlett, and others have argued generally, and Karma Lochrie has argued particularly in terms of Margery Kempe, there were varying degrees of "literate" ability in pre-modern England. Margery, for example, could have been able to read, but not write. She might have had some reading ability in the vernacular (although probably not Latin). It is likely she had access to texts through friends or relatives who could read (or even write). Harding argues that Margery's "illiteracy" liberates her from having to communicate through patriarchal discourse, which, given what I consider to be inconclusive evidence to Margery's complete illiteracy, is perhaps too sweeping a claim for Margery's separation from patriarchal discourse. Lochrie, in her very important book, argues for a closer look at both the variations in access to texts and "literacy" in general, as well as the cultural situation of Margery as laywoman and mystic in particular to reassess her authority over her text. See Wendy Harding, "Body into Text: *The Book of Margery Kempe*" in *Feminist Approaches to the Body in Medieval Literature,* eds. Lomperis and Stanbury, (Philadelphia: University of Pennsylvania Press, 1993), p. 179, and Karma Lochrie, "From Utterance to Text:

Authorizing the Mystical Word" in *Margery Kempe and Translations of the Flesh* (Philadelphia: UP Press, 1991), pp. 98, 97–134.

[60] For a more thorough discussion of this complex relationship between Margery's "literacy" and the authority of her text, see Karma Lochrie, "From Utterance to Text."

[61] Harding, "Body into Text," p. 169.

[62] John Hirsch in his essay "Author and Scribe in *The Book of Margery Kempe*," *Medium Aevum* 44 (1975), pp. 45–50, argues that the scribe may have imposed order on Margery's text, editing out repetitions, and giving the text "direction" and therefore "should be regarded as the author" (150) as much as Margery. This, of course, is a common complaint about many women's texts-that they lack order and/or are repetitive or excessive, and require a presumably male intercessor to impose order and give "meaning" to the text.

[63] Margery of course is sent into rapture by many material presences, including sick people and babies.

[64] *The Book of Margery Kempe*, p. 198.

[65] All women remaining virgins would inevitably lead to the end of the human race, but theologians such as Jerome were prepared to accept this possibility: "Here our opponent goes utterly wild with exultation...If the Lord had commanded virginity, He would have seemed to condemn marriage, and to do away with the seed-plot of mankind, of which virginity itself is a growth. If he cut off the root, how was He to expect fruit?...The Master of the Christian race offers the reward, invites candidates to the course, holds in His hand the prize of virginity, points to the fountain of purity, and cries aloud "If any man thirst, let him come unto me and drink."...And therefore Christ loves virgins more than others.' *The Principal Works of St. Jerome*, trans. W.H. Fremantle (New York: Christian Literature Company, 1893), pp. 360–65. Reprinted in Robert P. Miller, *Chaucer: Sources and Backgrounds* (New York: Oxford University Press, 1977), pp. 415–436.

[66] As mentioned in Chapter Two, texts such as *Hali Meidenhad* and *Ancrene Wisse*, were devoted to evoking fear and anxiety among women about the evils of gossip and childbearing.

[67] *The Book of Margery Kempe*, p. 199.

[68] Ibid., p. 199.

[69] We can compare this to a similar moment in Julian of Norwich's *Book of Showings* in which images of fertility and barrenness are described in relation to prayer, and whether God will grant an audience: "...for we be nott suer that god heryth vs, as we thngke for oure vnwurthynesse and for we fele ryght nought: for we be as bareyne and as drye ofte tymes after oure prayers as we were before" (460). Fertility is linked to a private and fulfilling encounter with God-or at least the sensation of being heard (i.e. possibly receiving the word of God).

CHAPTER FOUR: "WITH GRIEVOUS GROANES & DEEPE SIGHES": FEMALE TEXTUAL AND BIRTH COMMUNITIES IN *THE MONUMENT OF MATRONES*

[1] Joan Kelly, *Women, History & Theory: The Essays of Joan Kelly* (Chicago: University of Chicago Press, 1984), pp. 19–50.

[2] As of this writing, there are but two critical works that address *The Monument of Matrones* at any length. One is Colin B. Atkinson and William P. Stoneman's "'These griping greefes and pinching panges': Attitudes to Childbirth in Thomas

Bentley's *The Monument of Matrones*" (1582), in *A Journal for Renaissance and Reformation Students and Scholars* 21, no.2 (Summer 1990), pp. 193–203. The other is Charlotte F. Otten's "Women's Prayers in Childbirth in Sixteenth-Century England," *Women and Language* 16, no.1 (Spring 1993), pp. 18–21.

[3] All quotations are taken from Thomas Bentley's *The Monument of Matrones* (London: printed by H. Denham 1582), p. 2.

[4] There were several ostensibly female-authored midwifery manuals in the middle ages, including the *Trotula* and "The Sekenesse of Wemen." I discuss these, as well as other texts, at length in Chapter One.

[5] This is also true of some versions of Psuedo-Albertus Magnus' text *De Secretis Mulierum*, as well as more contemporary texts like Guillemeau's *Child-birth, or the Happy Deliverie of Women* (1612).

[6] Chapter One presents a fuller discussion about how men begin to infiltrate the female birthplace and how various texts played a role in this shift.

[7] In the Introduction I examine the complex nature of "literacy," and the methods by which information could have been disseminated.

[8] For example, in the mid-seventeenth century Lady Grace Mildmay had a compilation of her medical remedies and recipes published posthumously by her daughter, and Jane Sharp published *The Midwives Book* (1671).

[9] See Charlotte F. Otten, *English Women's Voices: 1540–1700* (Miami: Florida International University Press, 1992), p. 173. See also my article, "'be unto me like a precious balm': Lady Grace Milmday, Sixteenth-Century Female Practioner," in *Dynamis: International Journal of the History of Science and Medicine* 19, (June 1999).

[10] Charlotte F.Otten in her essay "Women's Prayers," pp. 18–21, argues this.

[11] In fact, during the early sixteenth century, on the heels of ever-growing popularity in the late middle ages, new festivals of the Virgin were being constructed by remaining Catholics. In addition, both Mary and her mother, St. Anne, were essentially patron saints of childbirth and safe delivery. See Jacques Gelis, *The History of Childbirth: Fertility, Pregnancy, and Birth in Early Modern Europe*, trans. Rosemary Morris. (Boston: Northeastern University Press, 19 91), pp. 145–160.

[12] One among I am sure many exceptions, is Elizabeth Grymeston's *Miscelanea, Meditations, Memoratives* (1604) which is quite "Catholic" in its imagery. Grymeston, like other female authors of "advice" books of her time, was concerned with the appropriate religious upbringing of her children (she had nine, but only one survived infancy). Her text is addressed to her son in the face of her death, and on how he should best handle "the houre of thy mariage, and at the houre of thy death" (A3r). It is replete with images of fertility and birth; she "resolved to breake the barren soile of my fruitless brain" (A3v) to produce this text. Her focus on the body as metaphor suggests her Catholicism. This text, in addition to other similar works by women, including Dorothy Leigh's *Mothers Blessing* (1616), and Elizabeth Joceline's *The Mothers Legacie to Her Unborne Childe* (1624) (Joceline did, prophetically, die in the birth of her first child), is also useful in understanding the construction of female devotional and textual communities, but goes beyond the scope of this particular study.

[13] In this parable, Christ tells the story of the servants who wait for their masters to return from the marriage feast "so that they may open to him at once when he comes." Those who stay awake in wait for them, and those that follow the direction and desires of their master even when he is not home, shall be blessed.

Notes to Chapter Four

[14] See for example the various uses in Exodous 28:8.9, Job 38:3.1, Isaiah 45:5.17, Ezekiel 44:18.18, and John 21:18.33, to name but a few.

[15] See Exodus 25.37, Zechariah 4.2, and Revelations 4.5.

[16] Bentley's text departs from Luis Juan Vives' *Instruction of a Christian Woman* (1529), for example, which is considered to be one of the most popular conduct books for women in Tudor England. This text's primary focus is not necessarily on "instruction" or education (only two of the thirty-eight chapters are on the appropriate things women should read and study), but rather on how women should live. In some respects, Vives' work is an early modern precursor to Bentley's in that it seeks to lay out precepts for women's lives from childhood to widowhood, from what kinds of clothes to wear to private devotions and meditations. Vives work also comes out of texts like *Hali Medeinhad* and *Ancrene Wisse*, also instructional manuals for women (on the topics of virginity and anchorites, respectively, and women's behavior generally).

[17] Patricia Parker interrogates the notion of the copiousness of the female body (the pregnant body) and the excessive use of language in *Literary Fat Ladies: Rhetoric, Gender, Property* (London: Methuen, 1987), pp. 8–35.

[18] Bentley, p. 2.

[19] Sexualized images of Christ the bridegroom can be found in later medieval texts that describe female mystical experiences of the body of Christ, particularly in *The Book of Margery Kempe*, as discussed in my Chapter Three.

[20] Bentley, p. 2.

[21] Genesis 1:28: "And God blessed them, and God said to them, 'Be fruitful and multiply, and fill the earth and subdue it.'"

[22] Bentley, p. 2.

[23] See, for example, the medieval *The Castle of Perseverance*, and George Herbert's *The Temple*.

[24] Bentley, p. 3r.

[25] See for example her self-representation as a Prince in her "Speech to the Troops at Tilsbury" (1588).

[26] travails

[27] Bentley, p. 3.

[28] Ibid., B1.

[29] Ibid., B1.

[30] Ibid., B1.

[31] Ibid., B8.

[32] Ibid., p. 123.

[33] Ibid., A-A.1.

[34] Ibid., Hh.ii.

[35] Ibid., p. 1.

[36] Ibid., B1.

[37] Raynald, in his Preface to *The Byrth of Mankynde*, focuses on the profitable nature of his text. I might also add that these kinds of texts, texts that promise to reveal the secrets of women's bodies, often practice a kind of commodification of women's bodily experience of birth, and even the particular language or birth (gossip).

[38] Bentley, p. 1.

[39] Ibid., p. 95.

⁴⁰ See Genesis 20:15 and 21:1 for the story of how and why God "gives" Sarah and Abraham a son at age 90 and 100 respectively. See also Genesis 25:21 where Isaac prays to God to make his wife Rebekah fertile, and Genesis 29:31 in which God "opens" Leah's womb so that she may bear children. Finally, see Luke 1:7 for the story of Elizabeth's barrenness.

⁴¹ Bentley, p. 95.

⁴² Ibid., p. 96.

⁴³ The devotional content varies from prayer to prayer in that while they are clearly all prayers and seek to address God, a few very consciously and specifically use the Psalms as their base, explicitly connect deliverance with childbirth. In this section, several Psalms are recommended for comfort, the "6, 38, 51, 102, 30, and 142 Psalmes of Dauid." One, Psalm 22, is printed here in Lamp Five, and is reformulated to account for the female voice that utters it, and the particular occasion of childbirth:

> My God, my God, why hast thou forsaken me. It seemeth that I shall not obteine deliuerance, though I seek in with lowd cries. My God, I will crie all the daie long, but thou wilt not answer; and all the night long I make pitious mone, without taking anie rest...(109)

The entirety of the prayer takes these kinds of liberties, which give devotional insights into the despair of birth (which is supported in the many other prayers), and which highlight the powerful relationship between delivery and deliverance.

⁴⁴ Elaine Scarry, *The Body in Pain: The Making and Unmaking of the World* (Oxford: Oxford University Press, 1985), p. 4. In the introduction to her book, Scarry writes about the nature of pain, describing it as that which "takes no object" and "resists objectification in language" (5). Her larger argument takes up the political and "perceptual" complications that arise from this difficulty (resulting in "unmaking"), and the philosophic "nature of human creation" (or "making").

⁴⁵ Ibid., p. 2.

⁴⁶ Ibid., p. 192.

⁴⁷ Bentley, p. 112.

⁴⁸ Ibid., p. 115.

⁴⁹ Ibid., p. 112.

⁵⁰ Ibid., p. 113.

⁵¹ This is a common image in both Margery's and Julian's descriptions of themselves, as well as in other descriptions of female mystical experiences such as those of Elizabeth of Spalbeck, Christina of Miribeles, and Mary of Oignes.

⁵² Bentley, pp. 112–113.

⁵³ Ibid., p. 113.

⁵⁴ Ibid., p. 113.

⁵⁵ Ibid., p. 113.

⁵⁶ Ibid., p. 113.

⁵⁷ Ibid., p. 114.

⁵⁸ Ibid., p. 114.

⁵⁹ Carolyn Walker Bynum in her seminal work *Jesus as Mother: Studies in the Spirituality of the High Middle Ages* (Berkeley: University of California Press, 1982) argues, among other things, that the emphasis in God as mother and father, friend and spouse was produced though the course of twelfth- and thirteenth- century religious changes in devotional practice. These practices of mysticism empha-

Notes to Chapter Four

sized the humanity of Christ; women would meditate and sometime reenact the physical ecstasies that accompanied his birth, life, and death. Some of these practices carried into sixteenth- century women's devotional beliefs.

[60] Bentley, p. 114.

[61] There are a series of prayers that are specifically directed for use by a "Queene, Noble woman, or Ladie with child" (129). The idea that a few of these prayers are specifically intended for a Queen, noble woman, or Lady, suggests that these women had, or at any rate were thought or desired to have had, different needs and relationships with God relative to what would generally be considered an "even playing ground." Again, while it is beyond the scope of this chapter to investigate what these prayers suggest about Bentley's (or the culture's) desire for Queen Elizabeth to get married and create successors to the throne, these prayers at minimum highlight the ways in which the patriarchal voice desires to infiltrate and speak for the female body in childbirth. It is, like the "revealing" of female "secrets" of anatomy and the mission of some texts like *The Byrth of Mankynde* to create anxiety in pregnant women over their midwives, a method of infiltrating an exclusively female experience and domain. The two prayers intended for a queen or noble woman make more specific requests upon God on behalf of the child, suggesting a concern over heirs. Also, and perhaps more importantly, these prayers appear as prayers for a laboring queen, rather than *by* a laboring queen (as a general rule, the prayers for laboring women are in the "voice" of the woman in labor). There may have originally been more, as the first prayer suggests by its heading: "Another praier for a Queene being with child" (128). But this heading also suggests, along with the voice not being that of the laboring queen, that this is yet another register of desire for Queen Elizabeth, or any Queen for that matter, to in fact be with child. This notion is bolstered by the reference in the very first line to the Virgin Mary (who is not explicitly mentioned in the other prayers), after whom Elizabeth consciously modeled herself:

> Almightie father, in whose favour the virgin Marie was higlie blessed among women, by the birth of Christ thine onlie Sonne our saviour, who also by thine omnipotent power, didst safelie deliver both hir, and hir cousin Elizabeth, and also mightilie deliveredst the Prophet, Jonas out of the whales bellie (128–129).

Here, as in so many of the other prayers, God is described as the agent of delivery. Yet in this prayer, more so than in any other prayer, the text actually lists the births God has attended. And, while his delivery of Mary is alluded to in other prayers (in a prelapsarian context), God not only delivers Mary, who serves as an image for Elizabeth, but he also delivers Elizabeth, John the Baptist's mother, and Jonas from the belly of the whale, as well! The result is one which constructs the Queen as hand-picked by God not only to give birth, because many of the other prayers suggest that all women's wombs are "fructified" by God, but hand-picked to rule and to provide heirs.

[62] Bentley, p. 134.
[63] Ibid., p. 134.
[64] Ibid., p. 134.
[65] Ibid., p. 134.
[66] Ibid., p. 135.

[67] *Rose Garden* and the later English version, *Byrth*, both have sections that address the problem of midwives. In *Rose Garden*, the opening poem expresses the following sentiment:

> In thought and feeling I contend
> That we must work without an end
> Whene'er a newborn's brought to light
> To save its soul with all our might
> ... For what God gives us with such care
> That we destroy it totally
> And such great things go unperceived
> Imean the midwives each and all
> Who know so little of their call
> That through neglect and oversight
> They destroy children far and wide
> And work such evil industry
> That they take life while doing their duty
> And earn from this a handsome fee. (Arons 34)

Later, in *The Midwives Book* (1671), Jane Sharp expresses a similar anxiety in her preface: "Sisters,—I have often sate down sad in consideration of the many miseries women endure in the hands of unskilful midwives; many professing they are (without any skill in anatomy, which is the principal part effectually necessary for a midwife) merely for lucre's sake" (1).

[68] Bentley, p. 135.

[69] Ibid., p. 139.

Select Bibliography

PRIMARY SOURCES

Albertus Magnus (pseudonym). *Women's Secrets*. Translated by Helen Rodnite Lemay. Albany: New York State University Press, 1992.
———. *De secretis mulierum or The Mysteries of Human Generation Fully Revealed*. Translated by John Quincy. London: E. Curll, 1725.
———. *Les Admirables Secrets d'Albert le Grand*. Cologne: chez le dispensateur des secrets, 1706.
Ancrene Wisse. Edited by J.R.R. Tolkein. EETS 249. London: Oxford University Press, 1962.
Aquinas, Thomas. *Summa Theologica*, Ia pars, vol. 13. New York and London: Blackfriars and Mcgraw Hill, 1963.
Aristotle. *Phisica, De cailo, De generatione et corruptione*. Translated by J.A. Smith. *The Works of Aristotle Translated into English*, volume II. Oxford: Clarendon, 1931.
Augustine, St. *Concerning the City of God Against the Pagans*. Translated by H. Bettenson. Harmondsworth, Middlesex: Penguin Books, 1984.
Bentley, Thomas. *The Monument of Matrones*. London, 1582.
Bonaventure, St. *The Journey of the Mind to God*. Translated by Philotheus Boehner, Edited by Stephen F. Brown. Indianapolis: Hackett Publishing, 1993.
Chamberlen, Hugh, trans. *The Diseases of Women with Child*. 1672, 1683.
Chaucer, Geoffrey. *The Riverside Chaucer*, 3rd ed., Edited by F.N. Robinson. Boston: Houghton Mifflin, 1987.
Galen, Claudius. *On the Natural Faculties*. Translated by Arthur John Brock, Edited by Loeb. London: Heinemann, 1963. [*Galen on the Affected Parts*, Translated by Rudolph E. Seigel. Basel: S.Karger, 1976]

Green, Monica, ed, trans. *Trotula: A Medieval Compendium of Women's Medicine*. Philadelphia: University of Pennsylvania Press, 2001.
Guillemeau, Jacques. *Child-birth, or the Happy Deliverie of Women*. London, 1612.
Grymeston, Elizabeth. *Miscelanea, Meditations, Memoratives*, 1604.
Hali Meidenhad. Edited by F.J. Furnivall. EETS 18. New York: Greenwood Press, 1965.
Hammond, E.A. *The Medical Practitioners of Medieval England*. (1965) (bibliographical register).
Hanson, Anne, trans. "Hippocrates: Diseases of Women, I." *Signs* I (1975): 567–84.
Henslow, George. *Medical Works of the Fourteenth Century*. London: Chapman & Hall, 1899.
Hildegard of Bingen. *Causae et curae*. Edited by Paul Kaiser. Leipzig: Feubner, 1903.
Hippocrates. *On Intercourse and Pregnancy: An English Translation of On Semen and the Development of the Child*. Translated by Tage U.H. Ellinger. New York: Henry Schuman, n.d.
Hooke, Christopher. *The Child-birth or Womans Lecture*. London, 1590.
Jerome, St. *Select Letters of St. Jerome*. Translated by F.A. Wright. Cambridge: Harvard University Press, 1980.
———. *The Principal Works of St. Jerome*, Translated by W.H. Fremantle. New York: Christian Literature Company, 1893.
Jonas, Richard. *De partu hominis* (1554).
Joscelin, Elizabeth. *The Mothers Legacy to her Vnborn Childe*. Edited by Jean LeDrew Metcalfe. Toronto: University of Toronto Press, 2000.
Julian of Norwich. *A Book of Showings to the Anchoress Julian of Norwich*, 2 vols. Edited by Edmund Colledge and James Walsh. Toronto: Pontifical Institute of Mediaeval Studies, 1978.
———. *The Shewings of Julian of Norwich*. Edited by Georgia Ronan Crampton. Kalamazoo: Western Michigan University, Medieval Institute Publications, 1994.
Kempe, Margery. *The Book of Margery Kempe*. Edited by Sanford Brown Meech and Hope Emily Allen. EETS 212 Oxford: Oxford University Press, 1940.
Kramer, Heinrich, and James Sprenger. *Malleus maleficarum*. Translated by Montague Summers. New York: Dover, 1971.
Leigh, Dorothy. *Mothers Blessing*, 1616.
Macfarlane, A., ed. *The Diary of Ralph Josselin*. London, 1976.
Mauriceau, Francis W.M. and Hannah Woolley. *The Accomplisht Midwife*, 1673.
Meades, Dorothy, ed. *Diary of Lady Hoby*. Boston and New York: Houghton Mifflin Company, 1930.
Parr, Catherine. *Lamentation of a Sinner*, 1545.

———. *Prayers or Medytacions*, 1546.
Pechey, John. *A General Treatise of the Diseases of Maids, Big-Bellied Women, Child-bed Women, and Widows*, 1696.
Raynald, Thomas. *The Byrth of Mankynde*. London: T.R., 1540, 1545, 1560, 1565.
Rösslin, Eucharius. *When Midwifery Became the Male Physician's Province: The Sixteenth Century Handbook: Rose Garden for Pregnant Women and Midwives*. Translated by Wendy Arons. Jefferson, N.C.:McFarland & Co., 1994.
Rowland, Beryl. *Medieval Woman's Guide to Health*. Kent: Kent State University Press, 1981.
Sermon, William. *The Ladies Companion, or the English Midwife Wherein is Demonstrated the Manner and Order How Women Ought to Govern Themselves During the Whole Time of their Breeding Children and of their Difficult Labour*. London: Printed for Edward Thomas, 1671.
Sharp, Jane. *The Midwives Book*. 1671.
Soranus of Ephesus. *Gynecology*. Translated by Owsei Temkin. Baltimore: Johns Hopkins Press, 1956.
Trotula. *The Diseases of Women*. Translated by Elizabeth Mason-Hohl. Los Angeles: Ward Ritchie Press, 1940. (*Passionibus mulierum curandorum.*)
Vives, Juan Luis. *Instruction of a Christian Woman* 1529.
Willoughby, Percival. *Observations in Midwifery*. Warwick, 1863.

SECONDARY SOURCES

Ackerknechy, Erwin. "Midwives as Experts in Court." *Bulletin of the New York Academy of Medicine* 52 (1976): 1224–28.
Aers, David. *Community, Gender and Individual Identity: English Writing 1360–1430*. London and New York: Routeledge, 1988.
Arons, Wendy. *When Midwifery Became the Male Physician's Province: The Sixteenth Century Handbook: The Rose Garden for Pregnant Women and Midwives Newly Englished*. Jefferson, NC: McFarland & Company, 1994.
Alexander, Michael Van Cleave. *The Growth of English Education, 1348–1648: A Social and Cultural History*. University Park: Pennsylvania State University Press, 1990.
Aston, Margaret. *Lollards and Reformers: Images and Literacy in Late Medieval Religion*, London: Hambledon Press, 1984.
Atkinson, Colin B. "'These Griping Greefes and Pinching Pangs': Attitudes to Childbirth in Thomas Bentley's The Monument of Matrones" (1582). *The Sixteenth-Century Journal: Journal of Early Modern Studies* 21.2 (Summer 1990): 193–203.

Aveling, J.H. *English Midwives: Their History and Prospects.* [1872] London: Hugh K. Elliot, 1967.
Ballantyne, J.W. "The 'Birth of Mankynde.'" *Journal of Obstetrics and Gynaecology of the British Empire* 10 (1906): 297–325.
Bartlett, Anne Clark. *Male Authors, Female Readers: Representation and Subjectivity in Middle English Devotional Literature.* Ithaca: Cornell University Press, 1995.
Bayron, H.P. "Trotula and the Ladies of Salerno." *Proceedings of the Royal Society of Medicine* 33 (1939–40): 471–5.
Beckwith, Sarah. *Christ's Body: Identity, Culture, and Society in Late Medieval Writings.* London: Routledge, 1993.
———. "A Very Material Mysticism: The Medieval Mysticism of Margery Kempe," in David Aers, *Medieval Literature: Criticism, Ideology, and History.* New York: St. Martin's Press, 1986.
Bell, Susan Groag. "Medieval Book Owners: Arbiters of Lay Piety and Ambassadors of Culture," in *Signs: Journal of Women in Culture* 7 (1982): 742–68.
Bennett, H.S. *English Books and Readers, 1475–1557.* Cambridge: Cambridge University Press, 1969.
Bennett, Judith M., Amy M. Froide, eds. *Singlewomen in the European Past, 1250–1800.* Phildelphia: University of Pennsylvania Press, 1999.
Bennett, Judith M., Elizabeth A. Clark, Jean F. O'Barr, B. Anne Vilen, and Sarah Westphal-Wihl, eds. *Sisters and Workers in the Middle Ages.* Chicago: University of Chicago Press, 1989.
Bennett, Tony. "Texts, Readers, Reading Formations." *Bulletin of Midwestern Modern Language Association* 16 (1983), 3–17.
Benton, John F. "Trotula, Women's Problems, and the Professionalization of Medicine in the Middle Ages." *Bulletin of the History of Medicine* 59 (1985): 30–53.
Bugge, John. *Virginitas: An Essay in the History of a Medieval Ideal.* International Archives of the History of Ideas, ser.min., 17. The Hague: Marinus Nijhoff, 1975.
Bullough, Vern L. "Sex Education in Medieval Christianity." *Journal of Sex Research* 13 (1977): 185–96.
———. "Medieval Medical and Scientific Views of Women." *Viator* 4 (1973), 485–501.
——— and James A. Brundage. *Handbook of Medieval Sexuality.* New York and London: Garland Publishing, 1996.
Bornstein, Diane. "Women's Public and Private Space in Some Medieval Courtesy Books." *Centerpoint* 3 (1980): 68–74.
Butler, Judith. *Gender Trouble: Feminism and the Subversionof Identity.* London and New York: Oxford University Press, 1990.
———. *Bodies That Matter.* New York: Routledge Press, 1993.

Select Bibliography

Bynum, Caroline Walker. *Jesus as Mother: Studies in the Spirituality of the High Middle Ages.* Berkeley: University of California Press, 1982.

———. *Holy Feast and Holy Fast: The Religious Significance of Food to Medieval Women.* Berkeley and Los Angeles: University of California Press, 1987.

———. *Fragmentation and Redemption: Essays on Gender and the Human Body in Medieval Religion.* New York: Zone, 1991.

Cadden, Joan. *Meanings of Sex Difference in the Middle Ages: Medicine, Science, and Culture.* Cambridge: Cambridge University Press, 1994.

———. "It Takes all Kinds: Sexuality and Gender Differences in Hildegard of Bingen's *Book of Compound Medicine.*" *Traditio* 40 (1984):241–52.

———. "Medieval Scientific and Medical Views of Sexuality: Questions of Propriety." *Medievalia et Humanistica,* n.s.,14 (1986): 157–71.

Cavenaugh, Susan Hagen. "A Study of Books and Privately Owned in England, 1300—1450." Phd diss., Universtiy of Pennsylvania, 1980.

Chartier, Roger. "Texts, Printings, Readings." In *The New Cultural History.* Lynn Hunt, ed. Berkeley: University of California Press, 1981. 154–75.

Chedgzoy, Kate, Melanie Hansen, Suzanne Trill, eds. *Voicing Women: Gender and Sexuality in Early Modern Writing.* Edinburgh: Edinburg University Press, 1998.

Chodorow, Nancy. *The Reproduction of Mothering: Psychoanalysis and the Sociology of Gender.* Berkeley: University of California Press, 1978.

Clanchy, M.T. *From Memory to Written Record: England 1066–1307,* 2nd edition, Oxford: Blackwell, 1993.

Clay, Rotha Mary. *The Mediaeval Hospitals of England.* London: Methuen & Co., 1909.

Coleman, Janet. *Medieval Readers and Writers, 1350–1400.* New York: Columbia University Press, 1981.

Copeland, Rita. "Rhetoric and the Politics of the Literal Sense in Medieval Literary Theory: Aquinas, Wyclif, and the Lollards," in *Rhetoric and Hermeneutics in Our Time.* Edited by Walter Jost and Michael J. Hyde, New Haven: Yale University Press, 1997.

———. "Rhetoric and Vernacular Translation in the Middle Ages," in *Studies in the Age of Chaucer: The Yearbook of the New Chaucer Society* 9, 1987.

Cressy, David. *Literacy and the Social Order: Reading and Writing in Tudor and Stuart England.* Cambridge: Cambridge University Press, 1980.

———. *Birth, Marriage, and Death: Ritual, Religion, and the Life-Cycle in Tudor and Stuart England*. Oxford: Oxford University Press, 1997.

Davis, Natalie Zemon. "Women on Top." In *Society and Culture in Early Modern France: Eight Essays*, pp.124–51. Stanford: Stanford University Press, 1975.

Debus, Allen G. *The Chemical Philosophy: Paracelsian Science and Medicine in the Sixteenth and Seventeenth Centuries*. New York: Science History Publications, 1977.

Deanesly, Margaret. "Vernacular Books in England in the Fourteenth and Fifteenth Centuries." *Modern Language Review* 15 (1920) 349–58.

Dobson, E.J. *The Origins of the* Ancrene Wisse. Oxford, England: Clarendon Press, 1976.

Dockray-Miller, Mary. *Motherhood and Mothering in Anglo-Saxon England*. New York: St. Martin's Press, 2000.

Dolan, Francis E. *Whores of Babylon: Catholicism, Gender, and Seventeenth-Century Print Culture*. Ithaca: Cornell University Press, 1999.

Donegan, Jane. *Women and Men Midwives*. Westport, Conn.: Greenwood, 1978.

Donnison, Jean. *Midwives and Medical Men: A History of Interprofessional Rivalries and Women's Rights*. New York: Schocken Books, 1977.

Dresen-Coenders, Lene, ed. *Saints and She-Devils: Images of Women in the Fifteenth and Sixteenth Centuries*. London: Rubicon Press 1987.

Dronke, Peter. *Women Writers of the Middle Ages: A Critical Study of Texts from Perpetua (203) to Marguerite Porete (1310)*. Cambridge: Cambridge University Press, 1984.

Eccles, Audrey. *Obstetrics and Gynecology in Tudor and Stuart England*. Kent, Ohio University Press, 1982.

Ehrenreich, Barbara and Deirdre English. *Witches, Midwives and Nurses: A History of Women Healers*. Old Westbury, N.Y.: Feminist Press, 1973.

Eisenstein, Elizabeth L. *The Printing Press as an Agent of Social Change: Communication and Cultural Transformations in Early Modern Europe*. Cambridge: Cambridge University Press, 1979.

Erzgraber, Willi. "Problems of Oral and Written Transmission as Reflected in Chaucer's *House of Fame*." *Historical & Editorial Studies in Medieval & Early Modern English*. Netherlands: Wolters-Noordhoff Groningen, 1985.

Ferguson, Margaret W. "A Room Not Their Own: Renaissance Women as Readers and Writers," in *The Comparative Perspective on Litearture: Approaches to Theory and Practice*. Edited by Clayton Koelb. Ithaca: Cornell University Press, 1988, 93–116.

———. *Dido's Daughters: Literacy, Gender, and Empire in Early Modern France and England*. Chicago: University of Chicago Press, forthcoming.
Ferguson, Margaret W. and Nancy Vickers, eds. *Rewriting the Renaissance: The Discourses of Sexual Difference in Early Modern Europe*. Chicago: University of Chicago Press, 1986.
Ferrante, Joan. "The Education of Women the Middle Ages in Theory, Fact and Fantasy." In *Beyond Their Sex*. Edited by Patricia H. Labalme. New York: New York University Press, 1980.
Fisher, Sheila and Janet E. Halley, eds. *Seeking the Woman in Late Medieval and Renaissance and Writings*. Knoxville: University of Tennessee Press, 1989.
Flynn, Elizabeth and Patricino Schweichart, eds. *Gender and Reading: Essays on Readers, Texts and Contexts*. Baltimore: Johns Hopkins University Press, 1986.
Forbes, Thomas. *The Midwife and the Witch*. New Haven, Conn.:Yale University Press, 1966.
Fradenburg, Louise and Carla Freccero, eds. *Premodern Sexualities*. New York: Routeledge Press, 1996.
Garcia-Ballester, Luis, Michael R. McVaugh, and Austin Rubio-Vela. *Medical Licensing and Learning in Fourteenth-Century Valencia*. Transactions of the America Philosophical Society 79/6. Philadelphia: American Philosophical Society, 1989.
Gelis, Jacues. *The History of Childbirth: Fertility, Pregnancy, and Birth in Early Modern Europe*, Translated by Rosemary Morris. Boston: Northeastern University Press, 1991.
Gibson, Gail McMurray. *The Theater of Devotion: East Anglican Drama and Society in the Late Middle Ages*. Chicago: University of Chicago Pres, 1989.
———. "Scene and Obscene: Seeing and Performing Late Medieval Childbirth," *The Journal of Medieval and Early Modern Studies* 1 (1999): 7–24.
Gilbert and Gubar, eds. *The Norton Anthology of Literature by Women*, New York: Norton, 1985.
Glascoe, Marion, ed. *Julian of Norwich: A Revelation of Love*. University of Exeter, 1976.
Graff, Harvey. *The Legacies of Literacy: Continuities and Contradictions in Western Culture and Society*. Bloomington: Inidana University Press, 1991.
Green, Monica H. *Women's Healthcare in the Medieval West*. Aldershot: Ashgate Publishing Limited, 2000.
———. "Women's Medical Practice and Health Care in Medieval Europe." *Signs* 14 (1989) 434–73.

———. "Obstetrical and Gynecological Texts in Middle English." *Studies in the Age of Chaucer* 14 (1992) 54.

———. "Recent Work on Women's Medicine in Medieval Europe." *Society for Ancient Medicine Review* 21 (1993) 132–141.

———. "Documenting Medieval Women's Medical Practice" in *Practical Medicine from Salerno to the Black Death*. Edited by Luis Garcia-Ballester, Roger French, Jon Arrizabalaga and Andrew Cunningham. Cambridge: Cambridge University Press, 1994: pp. 322–52.

Griffiths, Jeremy and Derek Pearsall, eds. *Book Producing and Publishing in Britain, 1375–1475*. Canbridge: Cambridge University Press, 1989.

Hannay, Margaret, ed. *Silent but for the Word: Tudor Women as Patrons, Translators, and Writers of Religious Works*. Kent, Ohio: Kent State University, 1985.

Hanson, Anne, trans. "Hippocrates: Diseases of Women, I." *Signs* I (1975): 567–84.

Harding, Wendy. "Medieval Women's Unwritten Discourse on Motherhood: A Reading of Two Fifteenth-Century Texts," in *Women's Studies: An Interdisciplinary Journal* 21, no. 2. 1992.

Hellwarth, Jennifer. "'be unto me like a precious balm': Lady Grace Milmday, Sixteenth-Century Female Practioner," in *Dynamis: International Journal of the History of Science and Medicine* 19, June 1999.

Hendricks, Margot and Patricia Parker. *Women, Race and Writing in the Early Modern Period*. London and New York: Routledge, 1994.

Hindman, Sandra and James Farquhar. *Pen to Press: Illustrated Manuscripts and Printed Books in the First Century of Printing*. Baltimore: Johns Hopkins University Press, 1977.

Hirsch, John. "*The Book of Margery Kempe*," in *Medium Aevum* 44, 1975.

Horowitz, Maryanne Cline. "Aristotle and Women." *Journal of the History of Biology* 9 (1976): 183–213.

Houston, R.A. *Literacy in Early Modern Europe*, London: Longman, 1988.

Hudson, Anne. *The Premature Reformation: Wycliffite Texts and Lollard History*. Oxford: Calrendon Press, 1988.

Hughes, Muriel Joy. *Women Healers in Medieval Life and Literature*. New York: King's Crown, 1943.

Hull, Suzanne W. *Chaste, Silent and Obedient: English Books for Women, 1475–1640*. San Marino, Huntington Library, 1983.

Jacobus, Mary, ed. *Women Writing and Writing about Women*. London: Croon Helm, 1979.

Jacquart, Danielle and Thomasset, Claude. *Sexuality and Medicine in the Middle Ages*. Translated by Matthew Adamson. Cambridge: Polity Press, 1988.
Jameson, Frederic. *The Political Unconscious: Narrative as Socially Symbolic Act*. Ithaca: Cornell University Press, 1981.
Jordan, Constance. *Renaissance Feminism: Literary Texts and Political Models*. Ithaca: Cornell University Press, 1990.
Kaplan, Ann E. *Motherhood and Representation: The Mother in Popular Culture and Melodrama*. London and New York: Routledege, 1992.
Kelly, Joan. *Women, History & Theory: The Essays of Joan Kelly*. Chicago: University of Chicago Press, 1984.
Lagorio, Valerie. "Variations on the Theme of God's Motherhood in Medieval English Devotional Writings." *Studia Mystica* 8 (1985): 15–37.
Laqueur, Thomas. *Making Sex: Body and Gender from the Greeks to Freud*. Cambridge: Havard University Press, 1990.
Lavezzo, Kathy. "Sobs and Sighs Between Women: The Homoerotics of Compassion in *The Book of Margery Kempe*," in *Premodern Sexualities*, Edited by Louise Fradenburg and Carla Freccero. New York: Routledge, 1996.
Lindberg, David C., ed. *Science in the Middle Ages*. Chicago History of Science and Medicine. Chicago: University of Chicago Press, 1978.
Lochrie, Karma. *Covert Operations: The Medieval Uses of Secrecy*. Philadelphia: University of Pennsylvania Press, 1999.
———. "Don't Ask, Don't Tell: Murderous Plots and Medieval Secrets," in *Premodern Sexualties*, Edited by Louise Fradenburg and Carla Freccero. New York: Routledge, 1996, 137–152.
———. *Margery Kempe and the Translations of the Flesh*. Philadelphia: University of Pennsylvania Press, 1991.
Lochrie, Karma, Peggy McCracken, and James A. Schultz, eds. *Constructing Medieval Sexuality*. Minneapolis: University of Minnesota Press, 1997.
Lomperis, Linda and Sarah Stanbury, eds. *Feminist Approaches to the Body in Medieval Literature*. Philadelphia: University of Pennsylvania Press, 1993.
Lucas, Caroline, *Writing for Women: The Example of the Woman as Reader in Elizabethan Romance*. Milton Keynes, England: Open University Press, 1989.
Marland, Hilary. *The Art of Midwifery: Early Modern Midwives in Europe*. London, New York: Routledge. 1993.
Matchinske, Megan. *Writing, Gender and State in Early Modern England*. United Kingdom: Cambridge University Press, 1998.
McCash, June Hall, ed. *The Cultural Patronage of Medieval Women*. Athens and London: The University of Georgia Press, 1996.

McEntire, Sandra. "The Journey into Selfhood: Margery Kempe and Feminine Spirituality" in *Margery Kempe: A Book of Essays*. New York: Garland Press, 1992.

Mclean, Ian. *The Renaissance Notion of Woman: A Study in the Fortunes of Scholoasticism and Medical Science in European Intellectual Life*. Cambridge: Cambridge University Press, 1980.

Meale, Carol M. *Women and Literature in Britain, 1150–1500*. Cambridge: Cambridge University Press. Cambridge Studies in Medieval Literature 17, 1993.

Millet, Bella and Jocelyn Wogan-Browne, eds. *Medieval English Prose for Women, Selections from the Katherine Group and the* Ancrene Wisse. Oxford: Clarendon Press, 1990.

Mulder-Bakker, Anneke B, ed. *Sanctity and Motherhood: Essays on Holy Mothers in the Middle Ages*. New York and London: Garland Publishing, 1995.

Niccoli, Ottavia. "'Menstruum Quasi Monstruum': Monstrous Births and Menstrual Taboo in the Sixteenth Century." *Sex & Gender in Historical Perspective*. Edited by Edward Muir and Guido Ruggiero. Baltimore and London: Johns Hopkins University Press, 1990.

Orme, Nicholas. *Education and Society in Medieval and Renaissance England*. London: Hambledon Press, 1989.

Otten, Charlotte F. "Women's Prayers in Childbirth in Sixteenth-Century England" in *Women and Language* 16(1)19:1821.

Parker, Patricia. *Literary Fat Ladies: Rhetoric, Gender, Property*. London: Methuen, 1987.

Parsons, John Carmi and Wheeler, Bonnie, eds. *Medieval Mothering*. New York: Garland Publishing, 1996.

Partner, Nancy, ed. *Studying Medieval Women: Sex, Gender, Feminism*, Cambridge: Medieval Academy, 1993.

Patterson, Lee, ed. *Literary Practice and Social Change in Britain, 1300–1530*. Berkeley: University of California Press, 1990.

Plomer, H.R. "Books Mentioned in Wills", *Transactions of the Bibliographical Society* 7 (1902–4), 99–121, 115.

Porter, R., ed., *Patients and Practitioners. Lay Perceptions of Medicine in Pre-industrial Society*. Cambridge: Cambridge University Press, 1985, 129–44.

Rawcliffe, Carol. *Medicine & Society in Later Medieval England*. United Kingdom: Alan Sutton Publishing, 1995.

Riddy, Felicity, ed. *Regionalism in Late Medieval Manuscripts and Texts*. Bury St Edmunds, Suffolk: St Edmundsbury Press, 1991.

Robertson, Elizabeth. *Early English Devotional Prose and the Female Audience*. Knoxville: University of Tennessee Press, 1990.

———. "Medieval Medical Views of Women and Female Spirituality in the *Ancrene Wisse* and Julian of Norwich's *Showings*" in *Feminist Approaches to the Body in Medieval Literature*, Edited by Linda Lomperis and Sarah Stanbury. Philadelphia: University of Pennsylvania Press, 1993, 142–167.

Russell, G.H. "Vernacular Instruction of the Laity in the Later Middle Ages in England: Some Texts and Notes." *Journal of Religious History* 2 (1962): 98–102.

Salsibury, Joyce E. *Medieval Sexuality: A Research Guide*. Garland Medieval Bibliographies 5; Garland Reference Library of Social Science 565. New York: Graland, 1990.

Sanders, Eve Rachele. *Gender and Literacy on Stage in Early Modern England*. United Kingdom: Cambridge University Press, 1998.

Scarry, Elaine. *The Body in Pain: The Making and Unmaking of the World*. Oxford: Oxford University Press, 1985.

Scott, Joan Wallach. *Gender and the Politics of History*. New York: Columbia University Press, 1988.

Sharar, Shulamith. *The Fourth Estate: A History of Women in the Middle Ages*. Translated by Chaya Galai. London: Methuen, 1983.

Siraisi, Nancy G. *Medieval and Early Renaissance Medicine*. Chicago: University of Chicago Press, 1990.

Smith, Lesley and Jane H.M. Taylor, eds. *Women, the Book and the Godly: Selected Proceedings of the St Hilda's Conference, 1993*. Vol. 1. Cambridge: D.S. Brewer, 1995.

Stanton, Domna, ed. *Discourses of Sexuality: From Aristotle to AIDS*. Ann Arbor: University of Michigan Press, 1992.

Stock, Brian. *The Implications of Literacy: Written Language and Models of Interpretation in the Eleventh and Twelfth Centuries*. Princeton: Princeton University Press, 1983.

Stock, Phyllis. *Better than Rubies: A History of Women's Education*. New York: Putnam, 1978.

Stone, Lawrence. *Family, Sex, and Marriage in England 1500–1800* London: Harper Torchbooks, 1977.

Talbot, C.H. *Medicine in Medieval England*. London: Oldbourne, 1967. Series: Oldbourne History of Science Library.

Tarvers, Josephine Kosteer. "'Thys ys my mystrys boke': English Women as Readers and Writers in Late Medieval England," in *The Uses of Manuscripts in Literary Studies: Essays in Memory of Judson Boyce Allen*. Kalamazoo, Michigan: Western Michigan University, Medieval Institute Publications, 1992, 305–327.

Tucker, M.J. "The Child as Beginning and End: Fifteenth- and Sixteenth-Century English Childhood," in *The History of Childhood*. Edited by Lloyd deMause. New York: Harper and Row, 1975.

Traub, Valerie, M. Lindsay Kaplan, Dympna Callaghan, eds. *Feminist Readings of Early Modern Culture*. Great Britain: Cambridge University Press, 1996.

Van Gennep, Arnold. *The Rites of Passage*. Translated by M.B. Vizedome and G.L. Caffee. London 1960.

Webb, Diana. "Women and Home: The Domestic Setting of Late Medieval Spirituality," in *Women in the Church*. Edited by W.J. Sheil and Diana Wood, pp. 159–74. Oxford: Basil Blackwell, 1990.

Weissman, Hope Phyllis. "Margery Kempe in Jerusalem: Hysteria Compassio in the Late Middle Ages," in *Acts of Interpretation: The Text in its Contexts 700–1600*. Edited by Mary J. Carruthers and Elizabeth D. Kirk. Norman: Pilgrim, 1982, 210–217.

Wiesner, Merry E. "Early Modern Midwifery: A Case Study," *International Journal of Women's Studies*. 6, no.1 (January/February 1983): 26–43.

———. *Women and Gender in Early Modern Europe*. 2nd ed. United Kingdom: Cambridge University Press, 2000.

Wilson, Adrian. "Participant or Patient? Seventeenth century childbirth from the mother's point of view", in R. Porter, ed., *Patients and Practitioners. Lay Perceptions of Medicine in Pre-industrial Society*. Cambridge: Cambridge University Press, 1985. (129–44).

———. "The Ceremony of Childbirth and its Interpretation," in *Women as mother is Pre Industrial England: Essays in Memory of Dorothy McLaren*. Edited by Valerie Fideles. London and New York: Routledge, 1990.

Wirtjes, Hannede and Arn, Mary-Jo. *Historical & Editorical Studies in Medieval & Early Modern English*. Netherlands: Wolters-Noordhoff Groningen, 1985.

Yaeger, Patricia. "The Poetics of Birth," in *Discourses of Sexuality: From Aristotle to AIDS*. Ann Arbor: University of Michigan Press, 1992, 262–296.

Index

Anchoress, xvii, 30–31
everyday practices of, 32–33
Ancrene Wisse ("Guide for
    Anchoresses"), xvii, 24,
    26–32, 49, 57, 61
Anglicus, Gilbertus, 12–13
Aquinas, St. Thomas, 2
Aristotle, 2
Arons, Wendy, 10
Askew, Anne, 62
Aston, Margaret, xix
Augustine, St., 4

Baptism, 5–8, 15, 53–54
Barren women, 29, 60, 76
Bartlett, Anne Clark, xx, xxii
Beckwith, Sarah, xv, 27
Bell, Susan Groag, xx
Bentley, Thomas, xvii, 24, 61–88
Benton, John F., 10–11
Birth communities, xvii-xviii, xxii, 12,
    22–23, 50, 66, 88; *see also*
    Female communities
    male invasion of, 10, 13, 18
Birthing chair, 15, 20
Bonaventure, St., 4
Book of Hours, xxiii, 6
The Book of Margery Kempe
    (Kempe), xvii, 24–25, 42–61,
    63, 66

authorship/amanuenses' role,
    57–58
Christ doll incident, 54–57
critical writings on, 44
female communities, 49–54
female procreative body vs.
    virginal body, 44
female subjectivity of, 44
iconographic motifs of, 44
male intercessor and intruder,
    57–58
pain in childbirth, 45–47
reproductive discourse, 59
sacred and profane visitations,
    47–49
St. Anne, Mary, and Elizabeth,
    xvii, 49–54
social performance of birth, 50
social and visionary experiences
    of, 44–45
spiritual maternal paradigm, 49
Virgin birth, 53
worshipful wives of, 54–57
Book of Showings (Julian of
    Norwich), xvii, 24–42, 45,
    61, 83
family of the Trinity, 36–37
God as perfect mother, xvii, 33,
    36, 38, 41
infant as pure soul, 40

Book of Showings (continued)
    procreating/birthing female body, 39–41
    Revelation 15 and deliverance, 38–42
    Robertson's bloody garland, 35–36
    virginity vs. chastity, 34
Bynum, Carolyn Walker, xv, 27, 44
The Byrth of Mankynde (Raynald), xvi, xxiii, 2–3, 5, 10–11, 14–24, 44, 64, 73, 84–87

Carnal desire, 28
Caudle drink, 8, 52
Cavendish, Margaret, 66
Celibacy, 43, 58
Charity, 30
Chastity, 25–26, 61
    married chastity, 61, 66, 69
Child-Birth Or, The Happy Deliverie of Women (Guillemeau), 15, 64
Childbirth
    boundaries of language and, 46
    as collective female activity, 7
    literary scholarship of, xv
    patriarchal anxieties of, 6, 23, 29
    physical pain/fears of, xvi, 29–30, 39, 45–47, 65, 77
    reproductive unconscious of, 6
    rituals of, 4–6
    "sacred" birth narrative, 48–50
    social performance of, 50
    speech during/language of, 78
    Virgin birth, 53
    women's procreative duties, 28–29
Childbirth rituals, xvii, 1, 4–6,
    paradigm for, 6–7
    separation, transition, and reincorporation, 6–7
    social practices of, 33, 52–53
    social separation and, 7–8
Churching (sacred reintegration), 5–6, 9, 50

Colledge, Edmund, 38–39
Compendium medicinae, 12
Confessor, 47
Cooke sisters, xx
Crampton, Georgia Ronan, 39–40
Cressy, David, 5
Cult of the Virgin Mary, xxi
Cultural elite, xix

"Dalyawns" (dalliance), 25–26
De partu hominis (Rösslin), xvi, xxiii, 20–21, 64
Devotional communities, xvii-xviii, xxii, 66, 70
Devotional texts, xvi-xvii, xix 24, 70
The Diary of Ralph Josselin, 1616-1683, 5
"Did Women Have a Renaissance?" (Kelly), 61
Dinshaw, Carolyn, xv
Dudley, Lady Jane, 62

Enclosure, xvi, 45, 53
    sanctity in, 8, 26, 83
Erasmus, xxi
The Expert Midwife (Reuff), 15

Female anatomy, 1–2, 20
Female communities, 5, 15, 48, 88
    physical space of, 8
    power of, 53–54
    spiritual dangers of, 31–32
    spiritual maternal paradigm of, 49
Female devotional practices, 62, 66
Female literacy, 27
Female textual communities, xvii-xviii, xx-xxii, 5, 10, 12–13, 22–23, 62, 66, 71–72
Ferguson, Margaret, xv

Galen, Claudius, 1–2
Gender/sexual identity, 45
Gibson, Gail McMurray, 44, 55
Glascoe, Marion, 39–40

Index

Gossip, 5, 26, 31–32
  etymology of word, 7
Gossipings, 8, 52, 57, 84
Gossips, 7–8, 13, 47, 52, 55, 57
Green, Monica, 12–13
Grymeston, Elizabeth, 66
Guillemeau, Jacques, 14, 64
Gynecological manuals; see Obstetrical and gynecological manuals

Hali Meidenhad ("A Letter on Virginity"), xvii, 24, 26–32, 34, 40–41, 46, 57, 62
Harding, Wendy, 43, 46
Hippocrates, 1–2
Hutchinson, Lucy, 66

Isodore of Seville, 2

Jameson, Frederic, xvi
Jerome, St., 4
Jonas, Richard, 17–18
Jordan, Constance, xv
Julian of Norwich, xvii, 24–43, 45, 49, 57, 60–61, 83

Kelly, Joan, 61
Kempe, Margery, 24–25, 42–60, 63, 66
Kristeva, Julia, 45
Kurtz, Patricia Derry, 9

The Ladies Companion (Sermon), 5
Laqueur, Thomas, 2, 20
Lavezzo, Kathy, 56
Literacy, xvii–xix, xxii
  book ownership, xx
  readers and reconstructive readings, xxii
  Reformation period and, xx–xxi
Lochrie, Karma, xv, 11, 27, 44, 57
Lollard communities, xix, xxi
Lying-in chamber, 8, 53; see also Enclosure
Lying-in period, 9

McInerney, Maud Burnett, 33
Madrid manuscript, 10
Making Sex (Laqueur), 2
Male-midwives, 5, 10, 64
Male privilege, 16
Margaret of Anjou, 8
Marriage, 28
Married chastity, xxii, 61, 66, 69
Medicine
  classical traditions of, 1
  exclusion of women, 65
  Greek theory of, 2
"Medieval Medical Views of Women and Female Spirituality in the *Ancrene Wisse* and Julian of Norwich's *Showings*" (Robertson), 27, 35
The Medieval Woman's Guide to Health: The First English Gynecological Handbook (Rowland), 9, 12
Midwives, 4, 47, 50
  competency of, 64, 85
  complaints about, 86–87
  male-midwives, 5, 10, 64
  as paid function, 87
  role of, 1, 52–53
  souls of young and, 17
The Midwives Book: Or the Whole Art of Midwifery Discovered (Sharp), 4–5, 15, 64, 88
Mildmay, Lady Grace, 65
Miscelanea, Meditations, Memoratives (Grymeston), 66
The Monument of Matrones (Bentley), xvii, 24, 46, 61–88
  Bentley's framing of text, 66–73
  childbirth prayers in, 63–64, 73, 78–79
  female devotional practices, 62
  female textual/birth communities, 62, 66, 71–72
  labor pains and spiritual deliverance, 76–84
  "Lamps" or sections of text, 62–63

The Monument of Matrones (continued)
   maternity/motherhood in Reformation England, 62
   parable of Wise and Foolish Virgins, 67–69, 73
   prayers for midwives, 84–88
   reproductive unconscious in, 70
   women's devotional practices, 64–65
More, Thomas, xxi
Mortality rates (infant/mother), 46
Motherhood/maternity, 33, 35, 41–43, 62

Navarre, Marguerite de, 62, 72

Observations in Midwifery (Willughby), 5
Obstetrical and gynecological manuals, xvi
   emergence of, 9–10
   female readership of, 12–14
   medieval/early modern medical views, 1–4
   The Rose Garden and *Byrth of Mankynde*, 14–24
   social management of sickness/childbirth, 24
   Trotula and "Sekenesse of Wymmen," 10–14
"Obstetrical and Gynecological Texts in Middle English" (Green), 12

Parker, Patricia, xv
Parr, Katherine, xx, 62–63, 71
Practica secundum Trotulam, 10–11
Protestant devotional practices, 61, 65
Protestant humanism, xxi
Purification Day, 58
Purification (or churching), 9, 50, 59

Queen Elizabeth, 62–63, 71–72, 74

Raynald, Thomas, xvi, 3, 10–11, 18, 20–23, 64
Reader, xxii
Reconstructive readings, xxii
Reformation period, xviii, xx, 61, 65
Reproductive organs
   medieval and early modern medical views of, 1–4
   visual representations of, 2–3, 20
Reproductive unconscious, xv-xvi, 6, 70, 83
   dominant culture vs. female subversion of, 62
   Jameson's influence on, xvi
Reuff, Jacob, 15
Revelations of Divine Love (Julian of Norwich), 83
Robertson, Elizabeth, 27, 35–26
Roper, Margaret, xx
Rose Garden for Pregnant Women and Midwives (Rösslin), xvi, 5, 10–11, 14–24, 86
Rösslin, Eucharius, xvi, 5, 10–11, 15–18, 20, 64
Rowland, Beryl, 9, 12–13

"Same sex" theory, 2, 20
Scarry, Elaine, 45–46, 78
"Sekenesse of Wymmen," xvi, 4–5, 10–14, 18, 23, 26, 46
Sermon, William, xv, 5
Sexuality, 56
   male-formulated medical philosophies of, 1
Sharp, Jane, 4–6, 15, 64, 88
Social separation, 7–8
Socrates, 1
Stock, Brian, xviii

Tabulae sex (Vesalius), 2
Talbutt, Lady Ellenour, 4
Textual communities; *see* Female textual communities
Thanksgiving ritual, 9

Thornton, Alice, 66
Trotula, xvi, xxiii, 2, 4–6, 9–14, 18, 23–24, 26, 44, 46, 84

Vesalius, 2
Vincent of Beauvais, 2
Virginal vs. maternal, 30, 51
    Mary and Martha allegory, 30–31
    masculization of, xvii
Virginity, xvi-xvii, xxii, 26–28, 30, 44, 59, 62
Vives, Juan Luis, xxi
Voights, Linda Eshram, 9

Walsh, James, 38–39
Widowhood, 28

Willughby, Percival, 5
Wilson, Adrian, 5
Women
    authority of, 62
    as authors, xviii
    barren women, 29, 60, 76
    as empty/passive vessel, 4, 59
    literacy and communal instruction, xix-xx
    medieval and early modern medical views of, 1–4
    transmission of knowledge among, xvi, xxii-xxiii, 5, 13–14, 55, 65, 84, 88
Wroclaw manuscript, 10
Wyciffe, John, xix, xxi

For Product Safety Concerns and Information please contact our EU
representative GPSR@taylorandfrancis.com
Taylor & Francis Verlag GmbH, Kaufingerstraße 24, 80331 München, Germany

www.ingramcontent.com/pod-product-compliance
Lightning Source LLC
Chambersburg PA
CBHW070621300426
44113CB00010B/1616